*T*he national park system has within it the finest examples of America's heritage. Its parks are more than superlative scenery and natural phenomena; its monuments preserve historic, prehistoric, and scientific areas of great value. The stories of the nation's growth and ideals are told at historic buildings, important landmarks, battlefield sites, and in inspirational memorials. In all, they represent America's finest treasures—priceless values that are entrusted to the National Park Service to protect, interpret, and administer for the benefit of all citizens.

Our parks are special places. From the hazy depths of
Grand Canyon to the historic buildings of the present era,
we can appreciate the heritage of both our earth and our country.
Today, thanks to the establishment of a National Park Service,
we have preserved these special places for our own generation and
all future generations to see and enjoy.

Front cover: Views of thirty park areas; Page 1: Cemetery Hill, Gettysburg National Military Park, by David Muench; Page 2/3: Early morning at Grand Canyon, by Josef Muench; Page 4: Cliff Palace, Mesa Verde National Park, by David Muench; Page 5: Park Ranger overlooking Petrified Forest National Park, by Rick Obernesser.

The dedication on page 5, used on the title page of all Story Behind the Scenery books, was written, and initially used in 1967, by Merrill D. "Dave" Beal, who authored the first in this series, on Grand Canyon National Park.

This book is dedicated to all who find Nature not an adversary to conquer and destroy, but a storehouse of infinite knowledge and experience linking man to all things past and present. They know conserving the natural environment is essential to our future well-being.

NATIONAL PARK SERVICE
THE STORY BEHIND THE SCENERY®
by Horace M. Albright,
Russell E. Dickenson, and William Penn Mott, Jr.

Horace Albright went to Washington, D.C., in 1913, intending to work in the Interior Department for one year. By two decades later, he had helped establish the National Park Service on a solid foundation and had served for four years as its second director.

Russ Dickenson, a 39-year veteran of the National Park Service, served as Director from 1980 to 1985.

Bill Mott entered the Park Service in 1933, served as Director of the California state parks system for eight years, and is the current Director of the National Park Service.

Edited by Mary Lu Moore
Project originated and designed by K. C. DenDooven

NATIONAL PARK SERVICE: THE STORY BEHIND THE SCENERY. © 1987 KC PUBLICATIONS, INC.
LC 86-81514. ISBN 0-88714-010-6 PAPER, 0-88714-009-2 CLOTH.

Birth of The Idea

"The service thus established shall promote and regulate the use of the Federal areas known as national parks, monuments, and reservations hereinafter specified by such means and measures as conform to the fundamental purpose of the said parks, monuments, and reservations, which purpose is to conserve the scenery and the natural and historic objects and the wild life therein, and to provide for the enjoyment of the same in such manner and by such means as will leave them unimpaired for the enjoyment of future generations."

DAVID MUENCH

Today, at age 97, Horace Albright still remembers in great detail and speaks in loving terms of the system he helped establish. Born on January 6, 1890, he went to Washington, D.C., in 1913 to begin a career he had not anticipated. His achievements profoundly changed the concepts of preservation and appreciation of public lands throughout the world.

The seeds for the National Park Service were planted at an evening campfire in 1870 in the wilds of what would become Yellowstone National Park. Cornelius Hedges, a member of the Washburn-Langford party exploring this wild and unknown region, observed that it should always be preserved for the American people, never to

YOSEMITE NATIONAL PARK, Calif. *The essence of the park is embodied in the thunder of upper Yosemite Falls as it plunges 1,430 feet before continuing its wild rush to the canyon floor. Established as our third national park in 1890, Yosemite boasts waterfalls, great granite domes, and superlative high mountain valleys and peaks that soon became world famous.*

YELLOWSTONE NATIONAL PARK, Wyo.-Mont.-Idaho *The park is famous for its many natural wonders but it is Old Faithful that must be accorded a major credit for the area's becoming the world's first national park in 1872. Although overshadowed by this giant geyser, the colorful canyons, waterfalls, lakes, mountain scenery, and abundant wildlife help round out the wilderness symphony.*

CRATER LAKE NATIONAL PARK, Oreg. *Nestled inside the cuplike caldera of old Mount Mazama, Crater Lake is an area of many moods—sometimes calm and vividly blue; sometimes somber and brooding under low-hanging clouds. The gemlike setting of the lake, the story of a violent volcanic past, and surrounding forest slopes combined to bring about the establishment of our fifth national park in 1902.*

be opened to commercialization. From this far-sighted idea came the establishment of Yellowstone as the first national park in 1872, with others being created soon afterward, such as Yosemite and Sequoia in 1890—all carved out of the public domain. It was many years before the idea of a national park system would take form, but America had learned to protect and preserve its treasures. Other nations observed this experience and followed our example until there are over a thousand parks in better than a hundred countries today.

The National Park Service became a reality on August 25, 1916. From 1872 to that date there had been much discussion, but little action had been taken to organize a cohesive entity from the diverse reserved areas the United States government owned: some held by the Agriculture Department, others administered by the Interior Department, a few scattered elsewhere. One important milestone was the establishment of the Forest Reserve Act of 1891, when Congress separated the idea of forest conservation from national parks. By this law the President of the United States was given the authority to create, by proclamation, permanent forest reserves on the public domain, whereas national parks had to be established by Congress. However, this legislation did lay the groundwork for the 1906 Lacey Antiquities Act, which stated that national monuments could also be created by executive proclamation. In the years to follow, many areas that Congress rejected as parks were made monuments first and later converted to national park status.

In 1910 President William Howard Taft, following an appeal from J. Horace McFarland of the American Civic Association, sent a message to Congress urging the creation of a national park bureau in the Department of the Interior. Bills by Congressman John Raker and Senator Reed Smoot were introduced, but no action was taken.

After the 1913 inauguration of President Woodrow Wilson, Franklin K. Lane was named Secretary of the Interior. He immediately called to Washington a classmate from the University of California, Adolph C. Miller, to be his assistant. Miller accepted but asked if he might bring a young member of his staff to work with him. Lane indicated there was an opening for a confidential secretary in his office. However, when Miller asked me about it, I had reservations, for I had another year to complete before attaining my law degree. In the end, I agreed when I heard the magnificent salary of $1,200 a year and an opportunity to complete law school in Washington by going to Georgetown University at night.

Arriving in Washington, Miller and I were informed of the pressing problems of administering the national parks and monuments and the need for a bureau to devote itself to their administration. Before much could be done, Lane and Miller took an extensive tour of the areas and operations under the Interior Department while I acquainted myself with the history and structure of the department, its programs, and its procedures and met as many members of Congress as possible.

Shortly after Miller returned to Washington, President Wilson called on him to help organize the Federal Reserve system. In 1914 Miller resigned to become a member of the first Federal Reserve Board.

On December 4, 1914, I was summoned to Secretary Lane's office and introduced to a handsome, white-haired gentleman named Stephen Mather, who had been offered the position recently vacated by Miller. Lane told us to go over by the hearth and its warming fire and get acquainted. We talked until nearly noon of pioneer relatives in California, our days at the University of California, Mather's after-college activities and my year-and-a-half stint in Washington. We agreed that if we undertook this assignment, it would be a novel adventure for both of us—and a very short one, too! Prior to this time I had repeatedly stated that I was only going to remain in Washington until the end of the current fiscal year. My desire was to return to my native California, marry my lovely college sweetheart, Grace Noble, and go into the practice of law in Will Colby's firm in San Francisco.

DAVID MUENCH

INDEPENDENCE NATIONAL HISTORICAL PARK, Pa. *Independence Hall, long a symbol of liberty, marks the site of the beginnings of American independence. Constructed between 1732 and 1756, the building later became the Pennsylvania statehouse. In this building a document drafted by young Thomas Jefferson was read in 1776 and immediately adopted as the Declaration of Independence. Here also, the U.S. Constitution was drafted and signed in 1787. Other historic structures in the park include Congress Hall, where the U.S. Congress met from 1790 to 1800, and the Liberty Bell Pavilion, housing that revered symbol of American freedom.*

MUIR WOODS NATIONAL MONUMENT, Calif. *A shaded trail along Redwood Creek offers a cool and inviting stroll through this land of giants and into a virtually undisturbed primeval forest. With ancestors dating back millions of years, the majestic redwoods rise from trunks as much as ten feet or more in diameter to form a forest canopy high overhead. The area was designated a national monument in 1908 to save it from being logged. It is named after the famous naturalist John Muir.*

These men—Stephen Mather (left), Elmer Reynolds (center), Horace Albright (right)—were at the heart of the effort to create a dynamic National Park Service. Meeting in April 1924 at South Calaveras Grove, California, they could look back on eight years of intensive effort to bring this about. Reynolds, while not associated with the government, gave invaluable assistance through his newspaper, the Stockton Record, *publishing extensive accounts about the new park programs.*

After a few weeks Mather and I decided we would undertake this necessary and worthwhile challenge for one year. Mather was sworn in as assistant secretary on January 21, 1915. As Lane left the room he closed the door, but quickly opened it again to say, "Oh, Steve, I forgot to ask about your politics." We concluded that this remark assured us that we would not have to deal in partisan politics, that we could go ahead with a free hand. That fact, plus the sense of urgency we felt in allowing ourselves just one year in Washington, spurred our efforts. When the year was up, we knew we were close to reaching our goals and were becoming deeply involved with the future of the park areas. So we stayed on, Mather until his incapacitating illness forced him to resign in 1929, and I until leaving to go into private business in 1933.

It is a lofty but erroneous belief that Stephen Mather and I were great idealists, that we indulged in philosophical discussions and charted the ways we would carry out our dreams for the reservations under our control. There wasn't any magnificent master plan, only a series of problems that had to be solved as they arose. We improvised as we went along. We never had the manpower, time, or money to be anything but practical, pragmatic, and tireless. To accomplish our goals we discussed, compromised, cajoled, threatened, pleaded, and tried to stay at least a hairbreadth inside the law, but we always kept intact our honesty and our rigid standards for the park service.

In March 1915 Mather called a conference in Berkeley, California, so that we could become acquainted with our park superintendents and their problems. At the close we outlined an agenda for ourselves: get the Raker-Smoot bill passed to establish a park service bureau; set up a temporary organization in Washington with R. B. Marshall at its head to relieve us of detail work; stabilize the parks by bringing in new superintendents where needed; improve accommodations and roads, for we anticipated automobiles were going

GREAT SMOKY MOUNTAINS NATIONAL PARK, N.C.–Tenn. *The famous Appalachian Trail is part of a system of more than 800 miles of walking paths and hiking trails in the park. It winds its way along scenic highland vistas and through wildland sanctuaries of unspoiled forests and flower meadows, with visits to ever-present streams and waterfalls. Log cabins and barns in the park have been restored in tribute to pioneer settlers who carved out a living in the wilderness.*

SEQUOIA NATIONAL PARK, Calif. *The great crest of the Sierra Nevada forms the eastern boundary of the park. It is surmounted by Mount Whitney, rising 14,495 feet, making it the highest mountain in the United States south of Alaska. Many glacial lakes and the famous sequoia forests occupy lower elevations to the west. Sequoia was established as America's second national park in 1890.*

to have an enormous impact on the parks very soon; and enlarge old parks and create new ones. It was a big order!

We realized that to accomplish these aims we would have to have a well-planned, comprehensive program divided between the two of us. Mather was a public-relations genius. So he devoted himself to the task of making the American people, and especially their representatives in Congress, aware of their national treasures and why they should be administered and protected by a bureau devoted solely to this cause.

Mather traveled over 37,000 miles that year, preaching his gospel. At his own expense he employed an old friend from New York newspaper days, Robert Sterling Yard, to handle publicity. Soon floods of articles were flowing from Yard, the finest being the distribution of a national parks portfolio composed of a series of beautifully illustrated pamphlets. Yard wrote the texts and Her-

HOT SPRINGS NATIONAL PARK, Ark. *It is best known for its mineral-rich hot springs that are the mecca for thousands of health-seeking visitors. Forest-covered Sugarloaf Mountain makes up a large part of the park. The area was set aside in 1832 as the Hot Springs Reservation and dedicated for use as a park in 1880. It was established as a national park in 1921.*

CHICKAMAUGA AND CHATTANOOGA NATIONAL MILITARY PARK, Ga.-Tenn. *On the fields and hills of this park occurred some of the heaviest fighting between the Union and Confederate armies in 1863. Bitter battles made famous such place-names as Jay's Mill, Snodgrass Hill, Missionary Ridge, Lookout Mountain, and Chickamauga Creek. The park is composed of several detached areas and has within its grounds many of the 1,400 historic monuments and markers commemorating the battles. It is located in both Georgia and Tennessee.*

bert Gleason, along with an employee of the Bureau of Reclamation, provided outstanding photographs. These portfolios were mailed out to 275,000 people who had been selected as prime candidates to help in the forthcoming push for a park service. The cost of the mailing was paid by Mather and some of his friends connected with the railroads.

When Mather realized that the park legislation was going to be postponed until after the long summer recess, he took it in stride. He immediately made plans to take a party of influential friends on a pack trip into the High Sierra: from the Giant Forest in Sequoia National Park through the Kern River country to the top of Mount Whitney, and then to the Owens Valley

and up the old Tioga Road to Yosemite. Mather paid all the expenses for the large party, which included, among others, Frederick Gillett of the House Appropriations Committee; Gilbert Grosvenor, editor of the *National Geographic;* writer Emerson Hough; lecturer Burton Holmes; and park people R. B. Marshall, Mark Daniels, and me. We were given a never-to-be-forgotten experience, and he was repaid with invaluable help from the members of the "Mather Mountain Party."

Mather and I then made an extensive tour of the larger parks, most of which neither of us had ever seen. We also dedicated the new Rocky Mountain National Park. We came back to Washington both awestruck and imbued with a love for the parks that never left us. But the end of

DAVID MUENCH

NATCHEZ TRACE PARKWAY, Miss.-Tenn.-Ala. *By 1800 an old Indian trail, or trace, had become the principal route of foot travel between Nashville, Tennessee, and Natchez, Mississippi. With heavy usage the trail was so trampled that it became a crude road. In 1808 the federal government converted it into an important frontier road.*

The parkway is a protected recreational roadway that extends through large stretches of scenic and historic landscape and roughly follows the route of the original Natchez Trace. It was established under the National Park Service in 1928.

our one-year oral contract with each other was in sight. The vital legislation we had been promoting was again postponed until the new year, 1916. This would be an election year, and it wasn't at all certain that President Wilson would be re-elected, that Lane would still be Secretary of the Interior, that our friends in the Congress would still be there in November—or even that Mather and I would be retained.

I told Mather that I was going to resign and go back to California. I was adamant about it. He didn't argue with me, just suggested that we go to Hot Springs, "take baths, rest and talk out the situation." So we took the train to Arkansas. One day Mather suddenly exclaimed, "I've been bitten by an idea. Horace, go get married, enjoy the holidays with your families and then bring your bride back to Washington. Stay another year and get the Park Service created and organized." He was, as usual, most persuasive!

The new Sixty-fourth Congress convened in January, and we knew right away that there was an aura of success in the air. The members seemed to be more informed and ready to listen to us. We held strategy sessions with them, adding well-known conservationists, writers, and government officials to various meetings. A bill was drawn up: it progressed through House committee hearings rather smoothly and was passed. The Smoot bill did the same in the Senate. Then trouble started once more. Compromises between the two bills had to be forged, but frequent recesses of the Congress to attend Republican and Democratic conventions and then trips home to campaign were maddening. We were desperately afraid that if we didn't get the bill passed in this session, we might have to start all over again.

By midsummer Mather was getting discouraged and once again left for California and a pack trip with a group of friends. I spent every waking moment in Washington working out the compromises necessary for passage of the Kent-Smoot bill. It all came together on August 26, 1916, when both Houses passed it, thus creating the National Park Service.

I knew Mather would be coming out to "civilization" from the back country of the Sierra Nevada the next day, but President Wilson would not be signing any bills into law until several days later. Luck was with me once more. I happened to hear a clerk at the Capitol mention that the White House had requested that an Army appropriations bill be sent over for the President's signature. I quickly prevailed upon him to put our park bill with it. Then I jumped on a streetcar and raced over to the White House. There I persuaded Maurice Latta, the legislative assistant, to get Wilson to sign our bill along with the other. I added that I'd surely like to have the pen that was to be used in the signing. All these things were done that evening, and I happily wired Mather that we had *our* National Park Service.

The years of 1915 and 1916 had been spent primarily in securing legislation to establish the Park Service. Here we were, with the organic act signed but no real bureau to run it, and no appropriations. And we were faced with an election

THEODORE ROOSEVELT NATIONAL PARK, N.Dak. *The Little Missouri River flows through the park where the president once operated the Elkhorn Ranch. Alarmed over the disappearance of big-game animals in the area, he made the ranch into a sanctuary for wildlife.*

The Historic Sites Act of 1935 established "a national policy to preserve for public use historic sites, buildings and objects of national significance . . ." Under this policy many areas including Independence Hall, the Statue of Liberty, Harpers Ferry, and Fort Laramie were designated as great historic treasures.

DAVID MUENCH

DAVID MUENCH

that looked like a Republican victory. On election night, 1916, Steve Mather, Bob Yard, and I remained in Mather's home in a state of rigid suspense. Although we were so-called Teddy Roosevelt Progressives, we were pulling for Wilson, counting on a continuity of administration to see our plans through. Late that evening it appeared that Charles Evans Hughes had defeated Wilson. However, next morning came the news that California had gone for Wilson. He had been reelected, and the world was a rosier place for us! Our enthusiasm and plans for the future were instantly revived.

Just when everything seemed so bright, a series of catastrophies struck. Stephen Mather suffered a complete mental breakdown in January

DEVILS POSTPILE NATIONAL MONUMENT, Calif. *Looking much like a giant pipe organ, massive columns rise as much as 60 feet. Glaciers quarried away one side of the postpile. Although not unique, this formation is among the world's finest examples of columnar jointing in basalt. Vying for attention is nearby Rainbow Falls, with a drop of 101 feet carrying the flow of the South Fork of the San Joaquin River.*

ZION NATIONAL PARK, Utah. *After a winter storm East Temple reaches into the clouds, and the colorful red hue of the sandstone walls of Zion Canyon seems to take on added intensity. There is a sense of the spiritual in the quietness and beauty of Zion that is expressed in its name. Old ruins tell of a time when the area was the home of prehistoric Indians. The park is rich in the history of Mormon pioneers who discovered and settled the valley.*

1917. I was appointed acting director and had to remain as such for almost two years during Mather's recuperation. Three months later the United States was at war in Europe, with all the resources of the nation thrown into that effort. This had a devastating effect on our new service.

First of all, money was now more scarce than originally anticipated, not only because the resources of the federal government were being channeled into the war effort, but also because Congress had always been stingy with the parks. Each park area had received individual appropriations according to its needs or to the influence of a powerful personage or pressure group. Some, such as Hawaii National Park, received nothing. Without a bureau to operate the system or an appropriation for it, our hands were tied. Therefore, I immediately had to start scrambling for both.

After a bruising battle with several congressional committees, a National Park Service bureau was organized in the Interior Department and a staff in Washington was authorized. But only $500,000 was appropriated for the remainder of the fiscal year to run 17 national parks and 22 national monuments totaling almost 6,500,000 acres. Through the bitter experiences with Congress in 1917–1918, I learned that our ideals could not be translated 100 percent into reality by legislation.

World War I had other profound effects on the new Service. Personnel in the parks were being drafted or were enlisting, and there were no replacements. There had to be constant vigilance against attempts to exploit the parks under the guise of war needs. Just one example was the pressure exercised by the influential president of the University of California, Benjamin Ide Wheeler, to allow grazing of sheep in Yosemite National Park to provide food for the troops. We circumvented this by getting word to Herbert Hoover, who was in charge of the Food Administration. He somehow stopped this plan. We never learned exactly how.

Of course, there were other very urgent problems in the first few years. Organization of the

BRYCE CANYON NATIONAL PARK, Utah. *The park is composed of several large horseshoe-shaped bowls along the edge of the Paunsaugunt Plateau. Rising from within the bowls are thousands of pinnacles and spires, the results of erosion by rain, snow, and ice that melt away the soft rocks of ancient lake deposits. Iron oxides and manganese in the rocks create a fairyland of colors and forms. An artist who was asked to paint the scene said simply, "It can't be done!" Other features include a rich assortment of animal life that occupies the forested portions of the area.*

Park Service and the day-to-day operation of it occupied most of the remainder of my time. Extensive trips throughout the system to meet personnel, learn the problems of the individual parks, and inspect roads, accommodations, and a hundred other things (the conditions of which ranged from serious to worse) were sandwiched in between formulating policies that would standardize and facilitate future operations of the Service. Mather and I always felt that from the beginning a pattern had to be established that would serve as the standard to build on in the future.

Toward this end, in May of 1918 I went to Secretary Lane and suggested that a policy statement be drawn up outlining goals and standards for the new National Park Service. He agreed and told me to get it done over the weekend! Lane issued it as a letter to Mather, directing him to follow the points therein.

The major thrust of the statement was that "the National Parks must be maintained in absolutely unimpaired form for the use of future generations as well as those of our own time; that they are set apart for the use, observation, health, and pleasure of the people; and that the national interest must dictate all decisions affecting public or private enterprise in the parks." To this day this is still the philosophy.

We weathered World War I and its difficulties. In late 1918 Mather returned full time as director. He had completely recovered and was a dynamo of action and ideas. The basic standards for the park system had now been set, uniforms designed, and personnel chosen to care for federal property and the wildlife within. Many programs had been inaugurated to ensure protection for our parks. Now I felt I could resign. I did just that.

My resignation was not accepted, however. Instead, Mather's powers of persuasion convinced me to undertake the superintendency of Yellowstone National Park (which is the size of Rhode Island and Delaware combined) to make "an example park for the rest of the system." At the same time, I was to be Assistant Director, Field. Because Yellowstone was open to visitors only a few months of the year due to inclement weather, I would have the remainder of the time to work with Mather in Washington and tour other parks. Arno B. Cammerer replaced me in Washington, and I headed west.

DAVID MUENCH

YELLOWSTONE NATIONAL PARK. *The Grand Canyon of the Yellowstone River is a young valley, only a little more than 100,000 years old. Slicing its way downward through altered volcanic rock, the river has produced a colorful canyon of exceptional beauty. As though to give emphasis to the setting, the river plunges over a lava ridge to form Yellowstone Falls before continuing its turbulent course. To the Sheepeater Indians, Yellowstone was "The Land of Evil Spirits," and this strange and mysterious canyon was regarded with a mixture of fear and awe.*

CARLSBAD CAVERNS NATIONAL PARK, N.Mex.
Huge galleries, lavishly decorated with stalactites and stalagmites—some fragile and delicate, some massive— comprise the heart of this huge limestone cavern. Living in the shelter of the cave are thousands of bats that stream out in dense clouds at sunset in search of food.

DAVID MUENCH

Even among the triumvirate who were trying to operate the whole system, communication was difficult. As I was on the move so much, I carried a typewriter to keep up with correspondence. Cammerer ended his day in his basement, typing letters to us while Mather kept pen and paper in his coat pocket, writing when he had a spare minute. Budgets kept us away from the telephone and even the telegraph unless there were emergencies. Secretaries and duplicating machines were nonexistent. Expense accounts were jokes. We received $4.00 per diem for board, room, tips, laundry, and everything else while we were away from home.

When spending three or so months each year in Washington, sometimes I had to sleep in the attic of the Cosmos Club. Fortunately, Mather was independently wealthy and could do better, but he very often used his money to buy land or build a ranger clubhouse or provide other help for the Park Service when congressional appropriations weren't covering a project he felt worthwhile.

At the time, these difficulties made no difference to us. There were too many exciting things to do. We were consolidating and improving the older areas of the system: building roads and sanitary facilities, setting up museums and interpretive programs, regulating concessions, and rounding up sources of new ones where they were badly needed.

Mather was a public-relations genius, traveling continuously, feeding ideas and suggestions to us as well as rallying support and financial aid from companies and individuals to save or enlarge our holdings. Cammerer remained in Washington most of the time, working with Congress, formulating the budget, handling personnel problems throughout the system, and covering a hundred different, difficult areas of an administrative nature. His intense interest in forming the eastern parks was just one more job he took on.

When I was not working on every sort of situation on a daily basis in Yellowstone, my duties were to study the problems of other parks. I would recommend to Mather for his decision problems I could not solve on the spot, inspect new lands for inclusion in the National Park Service, fight off additions of unsuitable areas, and

Aside from a period in 1922 when Mather again suffered a nervous collapse and Cammerer became acting director, this was the team and the manner in which the National Park Service operated between 1919 and 1929. There was so much to do and so few to do it. Improvisation was our key word. There was little precedent to go by; there was not time for long conferences; and there were no experts nor money to pay for outside advice. We were fortunate to receive a lot of free consultation from some of the finest experts in the fields of wildlife conservation and landscape architecture, like J. Horace McFarland and Frederick Law Olmstead. Because of our limited budget we freely "borrowed" men on salary with the Geological Survey, Bureau of Reclamation, and other agencies in the Interior Department.

CHACO CULTURE NATIONAL HISTORICAL PARK, N.Mex. *About A.D. 1100, people of the Anasazi culture settled in Chaco Canyon and built a number of large pueblos. One of the largest of these was Pueblo Bonito. Farming was carried on in the lowlands, and for a time the pueblo flourished. Slowly, however, the people drifted away, leaving behind this impressive reminder of their former activities. Today the ruins are protected and stabilized.*

DAVID MUENCH

once in a while even get rid of a park such as Sully's Hill in North Dakota. I guess you'd say I was a roving troubleshooter.

In Yellowstone I found plenty of problems to keep me busy: from seeing that roads were watered down to hearing complaints from visitors about bears not standing still to have their pictures taken. On the side, I was writing articles for magazines like *The Saturday Evening Post* to promote our ideas. In addition, I entertained princes, presidents, and endless congressional committees. When Mather or a Secretary of the Interior

needed a study or report made, I usually filled that slot too.

As an example, in March 1920 I left Washington and, taking my wife Grace with me, sailed for Hawaii. Hawaii National Park had been established by Congress in 1916, a few months before the creation of the Service. But no funds were made available to pay for personnel, improve roads, prevent damage to natural features, or even settle the boundaries. In fact, Mather had been the only Park Service member to visit it, and then only briefly. Now I spent three weeks on foot, on horseback, or by car going over almost every inch of Haleakala on Maui and the Kilauea and Mauna Loa areas on Hawaii, which comprised the park, plus the spectacular wonders of Kauai, to evaluate whether they should be added.

Between trips to the various islands, I was in constant conferences in Honolulu with territorial officials and representatives of the Bishop Estate, with whom we were trading lands to permanently round out our boundaries. The Hawaii Tourist Bureau, which had helped so much in pushing through the original legislation for the park, now provided people to educate, guide, and entertain my wife and me. We came home confirmed Hawaiians. And because the Park Service was so enthusiastic and promoted their park (Haleakala was part of Hawaii National Park at this time) so widely, I always felt that we had had a large part in the future tourist explosion in the islands—for better or for worse.

GLENN VAN NIMWEGEN

YELLOWSTONE NATIONAL PARK. *Large numbers of elk live in the park and are frequently seen as early snowfalls force them into warm valleys.*

Immediately after the war there was a great spurt of travel in the country: "See America first." The automobile's popularity was the cause. Suddenly roads, food, lodging, concessions, sanitary facilities, personnel, and wildlife protection appeared inadequate or outdated. Camping by thousands of outdoor enthusiasts was a new phenomenon. Magazines and newspapers jumped on the bandwagon with pictures and articles to entice readers to visit America's wonderlands. And so they did—by the millions. They forever changed some wilderness areas into popular playgrounds. In the future the challenge would be how to preserve and protect these areas from destruction by those who loved them too much.

In this era of billion-dollar appropriations, it is hard to describe the fiscal situation of the National Park Service in the 1920s. To government administrators it was a time of tightly restrained budgets, difficulty with breaking from past traditions, and powerful individual congressmen who could make or break legislative acts with ease. The congressional committees granted money to the Park Service on the basis of how many people were using the parks.

It seems strange at the present time, when many parks are overcrowded, to recall that we were forced to publicize and to encourage people to come visit our areas by every means we could: "The more the merrier." It was the only way to get the financial help we desperately needed to build roads and sanitary facilities; hire more personnel to maintain the scenic, natural history, or historical treasures we held; and acquire all the additional areas we felt must be saved.

However, we did have other things going for us. The bureaucracy was relatively small, with fairly easy access to members of Congress. Many became close friends and confidants, giving us advice on strategy, pushing through legislation, and, most of all, getting us the financing we needed to carry out our plans. Senator Tasker Oddie of Nevada was one of these. When I was superintendent of Yellowstone, he asked to be a ranger during a summer recess of Congress. We couldn't say no, so he worked without pay and was an excellent ranger. He learned so much about park operations that from then on he was one of our most loyal boosters at the Capitol. Congressman Louis Cramton of the Appropriations Committee became such a devotee of the Park Service that he formulated policy, instituted plans

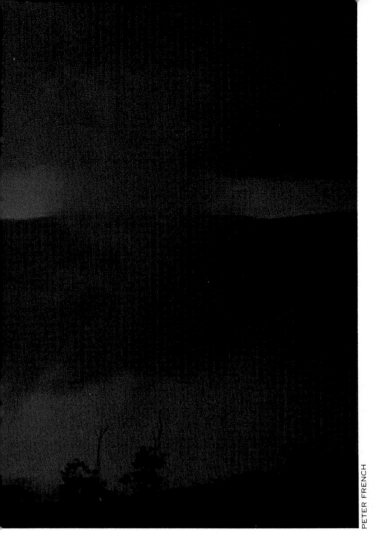

PETER FRENCH

HAWAII VOLCANOES NATIONAL PARK. *A volcanic eruption is one of nature's grandest and most dramatic shows. Like any good production, tremors and earthquakes herald the event. One or more fiery fountains rise skyward, sometimes reaching heights of several hundred feet. Seen at night, the spectacle is awesome. Incredibly, plant life soon appears among the cracks and crevices of the gradually cooling lava flows.*

for parks, and then never let up in Congress until they became a reality. He was our guardian angel.

We had been shocked by the relative ease with which Hawaii, Lassen Volcanic, and Mount McKinley national parks had been established prior to the passage of the Park Service bill of 1916. They had provisions allowing certain obnoxious operations to be continued: mining and hunting in McKinley; summer homes in Hawaii; railroads, reservoirs, and homes in Lassen. Some of these problems had been created because Congressman Raker had sponsored their bills as well as the one creating the Park Service itself. We didn't dare fight him, or we might lose everything.

In more recent times we have been criticized for not trying to preserve much more land than we did 60 years ago. Yet when you consider the fact that we had no professional consultants, miserably small appropriations, and influential park proponents, in and out of Congress, who saw nothing wrong with commercial exploitation of park resources and were mainly interested in tourist trade, we did manage to accomplish a great deal.

Keeping all these things in mind, Mather, Cammerer, and I stuck to our main principles:

HALEAKALA NATIONAL PARK, Maui, Hawaii. *The most beautiful and unusual plant growing in the park highland is the silversword. Living in and around Haleakala Crater, it may spend from 5 to 20 years before finally developing a stalk bearing a large cluster of flowers. A member of the sunflower family, the silversword produces hundreds of seeds.*

23

DENALI NATIONAL PARK AND PRESERVE, Alaska. *Mount Mather, named for the first director of the National Park Service, is one of several peaks in the glacier-clad Alaska Range that tower more than 18,000 feet, making this range the highest in the United States.*

Preceeding pages: GLACIER NATIONAL PARK, Mont. *A rich glow bathes the upper part of St. Mary's Lake as the sun sweeps under the heavy storm clouds and brings the colors of the peaks to vibrant life. There are many such lakes in the park, scoured out by moving glacial ice. Photo by Jeff Gnass.*

work out park boundaries on the most liberal scale possible and draw up legislation to prohibit activities inconsistent with our National Park Service founding act. Mather had started back in 1915, when he wanted to purchase the road over Tioga Pass. It had fallen into disrepair and could not be safely used to cross into Yosemite Valley. He met a wealthy friend from Chicago who asked why he had been in California. Mather replied that he was negotiating for an old mining road "which you and I are going to buy." "All right," his friend said. " I might as well agree to pay up now, because you'll persuade me to do it anyway."

In Sequoia National Park, the Giant Forest, with the tallest tree in the world, was in private hands but could be bought for $50,000. By the time Congress was convinced to put up the money, the price had been raised to $70,000. Gilbert Grosvenor of the National Geographic Society persuaded that organization to donate the extra $20,000.

We recognized that most of the areas under our jurisdiction were in the western part of the United States, while little of the power and influence in the Congress was from there. So there was a conscious effort to locate national parks in the more populous east-of-the-Mississippi region. Arno Cammerer played a key role here. He met John D. Rockefeller, Jr., in connection with a road problem in Acadia Park in Maine. They became good friends, and Cammerer interested him not only in adding lands to Acadia, but also in financially aiding Shenandoah Park and making possible the Great Smoky Mountains National Park with a gift of $5 million to match funds put up by the states of Tennessee and North Carolina.

I was also fortunate in meeting Rockefeller about the same time, but out in the West. This meeting would result in the saving of the beautiful valley below the Teton Mountains in Wyoming—an objective that had become almost an obsession with me. I fought for this goal 35 years,

DEVILS TOWER NATIONAL MONUMENT, Wyo. *Millions of years ago molten lava forced its way up under the earth's surface and gradually cooled. As time passed, erosion removed the overlying rocks, exposing the fluted columns of the tower. Early-day Indians held it in considerable awe and called it* Mateo Tepee, *"Bear Lodge." Because of its uniqueness and beauty, in 1906 Devils Tower was proclaimed the first national monument.*

JEFF GNASS

in and out of government, as the problem escalated from a local matter to a state issue, then to Washington, where Congressional legislation finally settled it all in 1950.

From the moment in 1915 when Mather and I first saw the magnificent Jackson Hole with its backdrop of the Teton Range, we determined to acquire it. Part of the area was under the Forest Service in the Department of Agriculture, but they never gave an inch without a fight. The remainder was in private ownership, ranchers predominately. Our first thought was to try to get the area added to Yellowstone National Park, which directly adjoined it, but this idea was finally abandoned after we met with bitter opposition. During a visit to Jackson Hole in 1926, I escorted John D. Rockefeller, Jr., and his family through the

LASSEN VOLCANIC NATIONAL PARK, Calif. *The Devastated Area was formed in 1915, when a violent explosion tore out the side of Lassen Peak, hurling red-hot boulders and sending a blast of superheated gases and a mudflow across the land. Trees as large as five feet in diameter were knocked flat as the blast cut a wide swath through the forests. Trees are now slowly reclaiming the once barren slopes.*

JEFF GNASS

area. This I had done with every person I could find who might help with the Teton problem. This time was the magic one.

The Rockefellers were overcome by the majesty of the sunlit range bordering the broad Snake River valley. Rockefeller asked me to prepare a plan for acquiring the private lands that faced an imminent future of logging along Jackson Lake and of mining nearby. Within a few months the plan was done, and a private company was formed to prevent knowledge of Rockefeller's involvement and thus keep costs within reason. Large tracts of land were then purchased by Rockefeller's Snake River Land Company. After President Coolidge visited the region, he signed a bill on February 26, 1929, establishing Grand

GRAND TETON NATIONAL PARK, Wyo. *A wilderness of wild, rugged peaks abruptly rises more than 7,000 feet above the windswept snow flats of Jackson Hole.*

DAVID MUENCH

Teton National Park. Compared to what we wanted, this was an insignificant area, but it was a start.

Through the years Rockefeller bought 33,562 acres of private holdings, at a cost of over $1.5 million, to give to the United States, but he held them until he could be sure the government was going to make a real national park from his properties. Time and again bills appeared before the Congress, politics ebbed and flowed, but always the results were the same: no park. Finally I suggested to Mr. Rockefeller that he inform Interior Secretary Harold Ickes that he would have to consider selling his holdings if the government was not going to incorporate them into a national park. This plan worked.

President Franklin Roosevelt bypassed Congress and created by executive order the Jackson Hole (later Grand Teton) National Monument (national parks must be created by Congress). This monument included thousands of acres from national forest and other federal lands, together with Rockefeller's possessions. It was still eight long years before a final compromise was made and a bill was passed by Congress and signed by President Truman in 1950. Grand Teton National Park then became a reality as we know it today.

In another area of preservation Stephen Mather really made his mark. For a long time he had felt that the Park Service could not, and should not, supervise all worthwhile projects for conservation or preservation. There was a great demand for adding new areas to the system by chambers of commerce, railroads, business enterprises of every sort, and hometown pressures on congressmen. Alternate methods of conservation had to be devised.

Mather's first move had been in 1918, when he joined Henry Fairfield Osborn, John C. Merriam, and Madison Grant in an effort to rescue the west coast redwoods from imminent logging operations. The Save-the-Redwoods League was formed, and it ultimately preserved a good portion of the California trees by purchasing large stands and incorporating them into state parks. Most of the money was raised from private individuals. Eventually the state of California took over many acres, while Redwood National Park became a reality for the federal government. And to this day the Save-the-Redwoods League is still receiving donations and buying redwoods.

His redwoods experience prompted Mather to call for a conference on state parks in 1921. It convened in Des Moines and, with the help of Iowa's governor, William L. Harding, attracted over 200 delegates from a majority of the states. Mather's desire was to establish a system of state parks in cooperation with the National Park Service. This would ensure that many lesser, though still very important, sites would be preserved and that the traveling public could stop each night within one of these sanctuaries. "A State Park Every Hundred Miles" was the slogan adopted by the conference.

A project that occupied an enormous amount

GRAND TETON NATIONAL PARK. *The towering peaks of the Teton Mountains dominate the land and tend to completely overshadow the Snake River, which flows through the park. It is along the stream, however, that other important values of the area are found. Winding its way through historic Jackson Hole, the Snake marks the wintering home of hundreds of elk. Moose, deer, and buffalo live in parts of the valley, while beaver work the river banks.*

DAVID MUENCH

BIG CYPRESS NATIONAL PRESERVE
Fla. *Lying adjacent to the Everglades is*
land of deep ponds and long sloughs
which exceptional examples of th
baldcypress tree are found. It is also hom
to black bears and the few remainin
Florida panthers. Since 1974 about on
third of the preserve has bee
administered by the Park Servic

WRIGHT BROTHERS NATIONAL
MEMORIAL, N.C. *An ancient prophet once*
said of men: "They shall mount up with
wings like eagles." Surely this must have
been the dream of the Wright brothers
as they gave wings to the nation and led it
into the age of flight.

EVERGLADES NATIONAL PARK, Fla. *Each year a feathered spectacle seen in the park during the dry season focuses attention upon the thousands of showy herons, egrets, eagles, spoonbills, ibises and wood storks. Less spectacular are the vast numbers of song birds and graceful flyers, such as sooty terns, that present the park as an exceptional world of bird life.*

of Mather's and my time was that of dealing with increased travel in the parks by tourists and with the concessioners who cared for them. After World War I most national parks had few or no facilities for the new wave of visitors. Mather insisted that concession "warfare" had to stop, that one concession would be granted for one type of operation in a particular park and that standards and profits would be rigidly controlled.

For the most part we succeeded. The railroads built new facilities, and bus lines were introduced for the first time. Lodging and food improved so rapidly that in some parks, hotels became world famous, such as Great Northern hotels in Glacier,

the Ahwahnee in Yosemite, the Canyon and Old Faithful hotels in Yellowstone, and El Tovar at Grand Canyon. New, less costly facilities ranged from log cabins to canvas-topped shelters with cafeterias nearby. Stores sprang up to cater to the needs of campers. Service was excellent because most concessioners employed seasonal college students who received very low wages but had the time of their life. The concessioners were helpful in attracting visitors and serving them well. In a great many cases they also became friends and allies of Park Service officials, spending their own time and money to help solve our problems.

ALASKAN AREAS. *Alaska is huge, and it has to be to include within its boundaries all of the National Park Service areas found there. A total of 22 units comprised of national parks, national monuments, national historical parks, and national preserves are scattered across the state.*
It contains human history—that of the long-ago migration of early man into North America and of the era of recorded events. Superlative wild scenery dominates the areas.

REDWOOD NATIONAL PARK, Calif. *Massive trunks that seems to reach into the sky are the hallmark of the redwood forest. Redwoods grow exceptionally straight and tower to a height of 300 feet or more, making them the tallest trees in the world. The presence of a heavy layer of insulating bark makes them remarkably resistant to fire. They also border on immortality, as they may live in excess of 2,000 years.*

To test his theories on concessions Mather picked Yosemite as the "ideal park." A bitter feud had developed between rival companies, the Yosemite National Park Company and the Curry Company. Although the original protagonists, David Curry and D. J. Desmond, were no longer involved, the rivalry was fueled by Mather and influential friends who put up considerable capital to help build hotels and camps for the Yosemite Park Company. Had Mather not been known for his scrupulous honesty, there could have been a good deal of trouble. To resolve the conflict, I was sent to force the two companies to merge into the present Yosemite Park and Curry Company.

JOSHUA TREE NATIONAL MONUMENT, Calif. *The Mojave Desert is the special domain of the picturesque Joshua tree, which is not a cactus. This tree-sized member of the lily family spreads across the land by the hundreds. Weathered granite formations in the Wonderland of Rocks area add a scenic touch.*

HARPERS FERRY NATIONAL HISTORICAL PARK, W.Va.–Md.–Va. *This quiet town was once the center of national attention before and during the Civil War. First came the famous John Brown Raid, whose participants seized the town and the U.S. Armory there in 1859. Later, because of its strategic military location at the junction of the Potomac and Shenandoah rivers, the town changed hands several times between Confederate and Union forces.*

Named for the first director, the Mather Training Center is used in the training of National Park Service personnel in the various disciplines essential in the operation of a park.

DELAWARE WATER GAP NATIONAL RECREATION AREA, N.J.–Pa. *Past generations of vacationers came to the water gap to enjoy its quiet beauty, and thousands come to do the same today. The recreation area includes 36 miles of the Delaware River as it flows between the Kittatinny Mountains of New Jersey and the Pocono Mountains of Pennsylvania. The famous Appalachian Trail passes through the area.*

Mather went on to build a beautiful clubhouse for the rangers with his own money and push through financing for a new post office and building to house stores. He promoted the construction of the magnificent Ahwahnee Hotel and lent his support to Ansel Hall for the first true museum in the Park Service.

Hall was a naturalist in Yosemite who, on his own time, had begun to collect specimens of flora and fauna, Indian artifacts, and geological specimens. Finally he put all these on display, along with books he had written to enlighten the tourists visiting the park. Of course, he very shortly ran out of space. Luckily, at this point he attracted the attention of the president of the American Museum Association, Chauncey Hamlin, who in turn engineered a grant of $70,500 from the Laura Spelman Rockefeller Fund to build a fine museum at the new Yosemite Village. The Rockefeller Fund later financed other museums in Yellowstone and Grand Canyon. Hall went on to be our Chief Naturalist for the Park Service, outlining programs for the whole system.

Two more divisions of the Service originated at Yosemite. When he was visiting Lake Tahoe, Mather encountered two University of California professors, Harold Bryant and Loye Miller. He was so impressed with their nature tours there that he talked them into switching the whole show to Yosemite. He would pay for it. So, in the summer of 1920, working under Ansel Hall, the

YOSEMITE NATIONAL PARK. *The inspiring beauty of Yosemite Valley, with its thundering waterfalls and its great glacial story, afforded a fitting place to inaugurate the first organized guided nature walks and campfire programs in the national parks. These popular activities gave rise to the Interpretive Division of today.*

two began day walks and nighttime lectures for the tourists. They were a smashing success, but the interpretive programs had to be funded for some time by private donations. This type of program is still the most popular in the parks today.

The other Park Service division that sprang from the extensive building program at Yosemite, making it a showplace for the system, was landscape architecture. As far back as 1915, Superintendent of Parks Mark Daniels had foreseen the need for competent landscape architecture that blended preservation with use. A division of the Park Service was set up as a model to supervise the construction of buildings and roads with minimum interference with scenery. This division was also to advise on scenic view points and indicate ways of saving as much natural growth as

possible. Of prime importance was the style of architecture for new buildings. It was to draw as little attention as possible to them, yet have them as attractive as possible. This style has since been recognized as "rustic architecture" and has gained a placed for itself in textbooks.

In connection with the rapid increase in automobiles during the 1920s and 1930s, we were faced with an incredible task of road building. Starting out with only one man to oversee these projects, within a decade we ended up with a full engineering division.

Some parks had roads that could be widened and straightened. Many areas had *no* roads. In Glacier National Park there was no way to get from the west side to the east side except to drive all the way around from the south. A wall of

(Continued on page 38)

Interpretation:
To See and Understand

by William Penn Mott, Jr.
DIRECTOR, NATIONAL PARK SERVICE

The pace of change across the nation is accelerating. Over the next 100 years most cities will have been so thoroughly reconstructed that current residents would find them virtually unrecognizable. Already a large number of us find a return to the places of our youth akin to a visit to a foreign land—or at least another state.

National parks are, at once, "special places"—living elements of their evolving worlds and islands of constancy amid the turmoil of change. The task of park interpreters will be increasingly important. It will be their job to help visitors see and understand the impacts of change and differentiate between the undesirable effects of human disrespect, like pollution and vandalism, and the acceptable, though not always desirable, effects of natural change.

Many of our policies are directed at long-term goals and are sometimes difficult to explain to the one-time visitor. Land acquisition, for example, is accomplished with heavy emphasis on allowing current owners to retain occupancy, knowing their property will eventually be available for public use. And we use a variety of natural processes to restore the park environment.

GOLDEN GATE NATIONAL RECREATION AREA, Calif. *Helping both young and old to have a better understanding and appreciation of the many aspects of Nature is the important task of the park interpreter.*

Such policies require wise, insightful interpretation. In time, as human impact brings ever greater changes around the parks, this task will become more complex than ever. We must continue the quest for complete knowledge and understanding of the vast web of life. The interpreter's task is still greater, for it is the interpreter who imparts to the public the knowledge and understanding we ourselves acquire.

It is sometimes said that park rangers are the last bastion of the Renaissance man or woman. In the midst of the modern information explosion, that is both more difficult and more important for the future. A quality interpretive program is central to the future of the parks. Because we have made a commmitment to the perpetuation of parks, we have also made a commitment to interpretive excellence.

GATEWAY NATIONAL RECREATION AREA, N.Y.–N.J. *Almost within the shadows of the city's tall buildings are areas offering excellent opportunities for those who wish to learn more about Nature and her many features. Every small pond, open meadow, or shrubby flat is an excellent habitat for some wildlife form.*

COLORADO NATIONAL MONUMENT, Colo.

The colorful red-and-buff sheer-walled canyons, the towering stone monoliths, and curiously eroded rock formations were virtually unknown except for some use by ancient Basketmaker Indians and later by Utes. Such was the situation when a wanderer named John Otto made his home in Monument Canyon. Greatly impressed with the beauty of the area, he built trails to vantage points and tried to interest others in his scenic wonderland. In 1911 he was successful, and President Taft designated the area as a national monument. Otto became its first custodian.

GLENN VAN NIMWEGEN

BADLANDS NATIONAL PARK, S.Dak.

Like the open pages of a book, ancient geologic formations are spread out for all to read. Softer rock layers are carved into a vast assortment of sawtooth ridges and canyons that support very little life. There are green areas where water is available, and here antelope and deer range, along with numerous birds and other small animal forms. An occasional prairie dog town may also be found.

DAVID MUENCH

HOMESTEAD NATIONAL MONUMENT OF AMERICA, Nebr. *The Homestead Act of 1862 threw open a vast prairie territory for settlement. Hundreds of Civil War veterans, immigrants from Europe, and families of ex-slaves took advantage of the new law and moved into the territory, building small primitive homes on their claims. One of these early cabins remain today as a memorial to their pioneer spirit and the rigorous life of that time.*

towering mountains stood in between. Our park engineers performed what is still considered an incredible feat by cutting the Going-to-the-Sun Highway through solid rock from Lake St. Mary's up to a 6,646-foot pass and down the other side to Lake McDonald—a 50-mile road on an awesome 10% grade most of the way.

Another wonder is the Zion–Mount Carmel Highway connecting Zion and Bryce national parks. This road boasts a 5,600-foot tunnel built through rock, with open windows that provide views of the spectacular canyon below.

We had to fight threats to almost every park region: commercial interests such as timber, ranching, resort construction, hunting, mining, and most of all—power and irrigation. In 1920 it took 17 pages in our annual report to list areas in danger. For Yellowstone alone, time and again legislation was introduced to Congress to set up dams, canals, and reservoirs that would have flooded great areas of the park. Two of the most powerful U.S. senators, Borah of Idaho and Walsh of Montana, were pushing these projects for their states.

On one occasion, after being ordered by Secretary of the Interior Lane to draw up a bill for damming Lake Yellowstone, I threw the only

copies of survey reports into the fireplace at the office and lit a match. The cleaning lady would "take care" of them. I also rather thought it might "take care" of me too, but it was worth the risk. These were the days before copy machines, and the government wasn't going to spend money getting a new survey made!

Another time, Mather and I agreed that we might have to resign if a certain water bill Lane supported passed. We never trusted him on this type of issue because he had been the man to seal Hetch Hetchy's fate, turning the sister valley to Yosemite into a reservoir for San Francisco's water supply. We were lucky that time, too, and never had to prove our point. Lane resigned instead.

Although Mather had suffered a slight heart attack while on a trip to Hawaii in 1927, he had not slowed down one bit. He held a superintendents' conference in San Francisco, participated extensively in the state park organization, followed closely the building of the Ahwahnee Hotel and the Zion–Mount Carmel tunnel road, and invested both considerable time and money in the upcoming election of 1928. On election eve he collapsed with a severe paralytic stroke. Cammerer and I rushed to Chicago. It was immediately apparent that Stephen Mather would never be able to resume the directorship, and I had to replace him. I was reluctant to do this until I could convince myself that this remarkable man might not be able to pull through one more time. On January 12, 1929, I was sworn in as the second director of the National Park Service.

At the time, the change seemed to have little effect on the Service. Mather, Cammerer, and I had long worked as a team. Although we deeply felt the loss of our inspirational leader, Cammerer and I carried on without a hitch. When I took over in Washington he retained his position as associate director and as my closest friend, confidant, and advisor. However, looking back now, it appears that Mather's departure coincided with the end of an era that was characterized by experimentation and organization and structuring of the system.

My directorship was the beginning of consolidation and of expansion into new fields. It coincided with a new administration in Washington. Fortunately I had known both incoming President Herbert Hoover and his Secretary of the Interior, Ray Lyman Wilbur, for some time and was on very friendly terms with them. Both were avowed conservationists and, as it turned out, were very helpful to me in the next few years.

Stephen T. Mather died on January 22, 1930. The previous fall, when he was passing through Washington, I had the Baltimore & Ohio delay the train he was on for a half hour so that the entire Park Service staff could go down to the rail yards to visit the old man. I spoke to him through an open window, even though he could not speak back.

During the years I was director, I believe that the National Park Service fared extremely well. Although the financial collapse and subsequent depression had devastating effects throughout the country, we received increasing appropriations. This was largely due to Congressman Cramton, who was chairman of the subcommittee on appropriations for the Interior Department. I had many other friends in Congress because I had traveled with them in the parks and had had

JEFF GNASS

FORT LARAMIE NATIONAL HISTORIC SITE, Wyo.
As a fur-trading post and later a military post, from 1849 to 1890 Fort Laramie played a vital role as an expanding nation moved westward. To take advantage of protection against hostile Indians, wagon trains passed by on the way to California and Oregon. Important treaties with the Sioux and Cheyenne Indians were drawn up at the fort in 1851 and 1869, enabling ranchers and settlers to move into the region.

Significant military history of the United States is preserved under a variety of titles, such as national military park, national battlefield park, national battlefield site, and national battlefield. These may primarily entail important structures like Fort Sumter, or they may consist of an extensive tract of land where a historic event took place, such as Custer Battlefield. The National Park Service administers more than 50 such areas.

DAVID MUENCH

CUSTER BATTLEFIELD NATIONAL MONUMENT, Mont.
A concerted effort by the Sioux and Cheyenne to protect their lands and preserve their ancestral way of life against encroachment reached a climax in June 1876 at the battle of the Little Bighorn River. Here about 225 men under the command of Lieutenant Colonel George Armstrong Custer were overwhelmed and destroyed by a large Indian force. Markers at the scene of the battle show where the last of the defenders were found. The nearby Custer Battlefield National Cemetery contains the graves of the identified dead.

to testify before them yearly on budget matters. Through these colleagues I accomplished a great deal toward meeting my main goals.

First we wanted to clear up problems within the existing parks and enlarge them. We put through repeals of old provisions allowing summer homes, mining, railbeds, and the like.

At this time new parks were either created or authorized, such as Carlsbad Caverns, Great Smoky Mountains, Shenandoah, and Isle Royale. Many monuments also were added to the system or were in stages of development. I used my summers, when Washington business practically came to a halt and Congress was not in session, to tour our existing or proposed park areas. In 1932 I spent many weeks just in the Southwest, on the lookout especially for sites to emphasize the role of Native Americans in our culture. By train, plane, car, tramway, mule, boat, horse, and on foot, I traveled down to caverns and canyons and up mountains; explored lonely Indian ruins; and hiked in places few white men had ever been. That summer I was in my office and saw my family for just 13 days.

This experience was not unusual, but it does exemplify the shortage of personnel and how we had to administer the Service. In connection with

BLUE RIDGE PARKWAY, N.C.–Va. *Two great national parks in the Appalachian Mountains, Shenandoah and Great Smoky Mountains, are connected by 469 miles of beautiful parkway. The road offers scenic vistas along mountain crests, travels through quiet rural areas, and presents in season a colorful array of wildflowers from spring until early autumn. Wild animals are frequently observed along the roadside and in the forests.*

National parkways are designed for recreational motoring rather than for high-speed travel. They have limited access and are landscaped and administered to preserve the historic and natural values of the regions through which they pass. There are four parkways administered by the National Park Service.

SHENANDOAH NATIONAL PARK, Va. *Viewed from above, the park presents an almost unbroken sea of rich green forest. What isn't seen are the many streams and waterfalls hidden beneath the forest canopy. The park is a delightful nature exhibit with flowering plants in abundance, a vast assortment of resident birds, and such large animals as deer and bear. It is truly wilderness.*

DAVID MUENCH

this, as we mentioned before, we had found that new divisions had to be added: naturalist, landscape architecture, and engineering. And after we entered the historical field, we introduced a chief historian as well as a historical architect.

———

While I was often engaged in following through with ideas that Mather had begun, I also worked on many of my own creation. As early as 1915 I had been thinking about the feasibility of the Park Service's acquiring not only the War Department parks but also monuments administered by the Department of Agriculture.

I had always been interested in American history and had given special attention to the few areas of this type under our control—all of them in the West. My opportunity to extend historic

preservation into the East came in 1929, when Mrs. H. L. Rust, a descendant of the Washington family, came to me for help. She headed a group who wanted to rebuild George Washington's birthplace, which had long since disappeared, in time for the celebration of his two hundredth birthday in 1932. They had bought back some of the original estate, and the War Department also had a small piece, but she needed an appropriation from Congress for the reconstruction of the house.

I seized the opportunity to enlist Congressman Cramton in the project. He persuaded the War Department to turn over control of its land to the National Park Service and then got a bill through Congress granting the money and the authority to rebuild Wakefield. I enlisted the help of John D. Rockefeller, Jr., and he responded with a gift that enabled us to buy 250 acres near the homesite. Wakefield was dedicated amidst widespread publicity. I wanted it known that the National Park Service had entered the historic preservation field.

During this same time, Colonial National Park was being created in Virginia on the peninsula bounded by the York and James rivers. Rocke-

JEFF GNASS

JAMESTOWN NATIONAL HISTORIC SITE, Va. *Only one original structure is left to document the story of the rise and fall of Jamestown. A few ruins remain to tell of its settlement by the first English colony in America in 1607; the fearsome events that befell them when many died of hunger; the Indian troubles; the destruction and later rebuilding of the town; and the heartwarming romance and marriage of John Rolfe and Pocahontas, the daughter of Indian Chief Powhatan. Along with Yorktown Battlefield, the area is administered as the Colonial National Historical Park.*

MARTIN LUTHER KING, JR., NATIONAL HISTORIC SITE, Ga. *A house in "Sweet Auburn" in Atlanta was destined to be the birthplace of the nation's most famous civil rights leader. It was in this community that he served as co-pastor of Ebenezer Baptist Church and expressed his strong convictions regarding the rights and dignity of his people. Later, in Washington, he was to electrify the nation with his "I have a dream" speech on the brotherhood of man.*

feller had already launched his restoration of Williamsburg, the colonial capital. Then, in 1929 an odd coincidence occurred. Unknown to each other, but almost simultaneously, Kenneth Chorley, chief of operations in Williamsburg, and Will Carson, chairman of the Virginia Conservation Committee, approached me with an idea to link Yorktown, scene of the surrender of the British, which ended the Revolutionary War; Jamestown, site of

GEORGE WASHINGTON BIRTHPLACE NATIONAL MONUMENT, Va. *Quiet charm marks the place where our first president was born. Meals for the Washington family were prepared in the Kitchen House, set apart in a separate building. On Christmas Day, 1779, his birthplace was accidentally destroyed by fire. Near the site, Memorial House stands as a tribute to his memory.*

The home of each president of the United States is a living part of American history. To preserve such sites, several have been designated as national historical parks, national monuments, or national historic sites. Here are found artifacts, exhibits, personal libraries, and accounts of the lives and administrations of our presidents.

the first permanent settlement in America; and Williamsburg. I was all for it.

I quickly secured the approval of Secretary Wilbur and President Hoover while Carson obtained agreement from the current governor, Harry Byrd, and the governor-elect, John Pollard. A conference was held in Williamsburg with all the interested parties present as well as Rockefeller and Congressman Cramton. A plan of action was agreed upon, and then Cramton went to work on the legislation. It took until 1931 to get all the details ironed out and the proper bills passed by Congress. The result can be seen today. Colonial Parkway joins Williamsburg (independent of the Park Service though linked philosophically) to Jamestown and Yorktown in Colonial National Historical Park. We had gotten a foot in the door, and now I aimed for the moon!

In 1933 Franklin D. Roosevelt was inaugurated as President of the United States. His new Secretary of the Interior was Harold Ickes, a notoriously bad-tempered, difficult man. I was sure my days were numbered as bureau chief. However, it turned out that Ickes had been a longtime

friend of Stephen Mather in Chicago, was a devoted conservationist, and knew all about me and our Park Service. The first thing he did was to assure me that both he and Roosevelt, whom I had known since 1915, wanted me to stay. I was honest with him, telling him that I was considering an offer in private business and would probably leave government service. But I would certainly stay long enough to see the new administration take over and to be a part of introducing my successor into the job.

In my consideration, Ickes turned out to be the finest Secretary of the Interior in terms of conservation, preservation, and national parks. I got along well with him as my new boss partly, I think, because I was one of the few who could pronounce his name properly.

It took a day-long journey to the Piedmont area of Virginia with President Roosevelt to seal the future of historic preservation. On Sunday, April 19, 1933, I joined President and Mrs. Roosevelt and a group of their friends and administration officials at the White House. A motorcade had been organized to visit Hoover's camp on

DAVID MUENCH

CUMBERLAND GAP NATIONAL HISTORICAL PARK,
Ky.-Va.-Tenn. *By following a well-worn trail made by migrating buffalo and deer, white men first found a way through the Appalachian Mountains from the eastern seaboard to Kentucky in 1750. Daniel Boone marked out the Wilderness Trail through the Gap in 1775, thus opening an easy route westward for immigrants.*

the Rapidan River to see whether the site was usable as a retreat for Roosevelt. Then we were to inspect the Blue Ridge Parkway, under construction, as well as Shenandoah National Park, authorized but not yet established by Congress. Although I had been assigned a seat in a car with several ladies (among them, "Missy" LeHand, Roosevelt's secretary), I ducked out and rode with Ickes, using the 105 miles to the camp to talk over current Park Service projects.

Once the party arrived at the camp it was quickly obvious that it was unsuitable for Roosevelt with his physical handicap. It was so hilly that several of us had to carry the President over to Hoover's house. After a delightful picnic lunch, we regrouped for the return trip to Washington. Roosevelt asked me to sit on the "jump seat" behind him so that I could point out interesting sites and give him information on them. As we rode along we got into a discussion of New York's Saratoga Battlefield, a site he said he had tried to

preserve. That was the opening I needed! I immediately poured out my idea of incorporating historic sites, battlefields, and other monuments into the National Park Service, and he instantly agreed with me. He asked me to have the outline ready and presented for his consideration as soon as possible. He added, "Work it out with Ickes."

I had already formulated a fairly detailed plan that President Hoover had presented to Congress in his administration. But after a Democratic legislature took over in 1930, proposals by him were consistently voted down.

Within a few days our plans were presented at the White House, and a sweeping executive order was signed by the President on June 10, 1933. This action made the National Park Service custodians of the parks in the District of Columbia and the national monuments then under the control of the Forest Service. Even Arlington National Cemetery was under our control for the time being.

With the passage of this act it was felt that the Park Service had solved many problems. First of all, the threat of consolidation with a bigger agency, such as the Forest Service, which had eyed us hungrily for years, had been avoided. Second, a balance had been achieved between East and West with regard not only to area size, but also to historic areas, now stretching from coast to coast, thereby increasing interest and financial support in Congress. And third, economy was achieved by consolidation of the administration of sites from three agencies into one. Our only regret was that the law changed the name of our Service to the Office of Public Parks, Buildings and Reservations. The change was reversed in 1934.

———

The next months were the most hectic, yet some of the most important for the future of the Park Service. With the deepening of the Depression, the desperate condition of the nation galvanized President Roosevelt into taking innovative steps. During the so-called Hundred Days after his as-

SHILOH NATIONAL MILITARY PARK, Tenn. *It is ironic that the name Shiloh, a biblical term meaning "place of peace," marks the site of one of the most important battles of the Civil War. It was around Shiloh Church that the battle began that was to rage for three days before the Confederate troops withdrew.*

ANTIETAM NATIONAL BATTLEFIELD, Md. *One of the most important battles of the Civil War took place around Antietam Creek, near Sharpsburg, Maryland, on September 17, 1862. The battle raged from early morning until dusk. When it was over, a staggering total of 23,114 men lay dead or wounded, making it the most costly single day's loss of the war. The battle was not decisive; the war would go on for two more years.*

THE WHITE HOUSE, Washington, D.C. *Major decisions of great import; personages of power, both national and international: all have made history behind the portico of the White House. The building has had a history of its own. Built on a site selected by President George Washington in 1792, it was burned by the British 22 years later. Rebuilt, it became known as the "white house" when its exterior walls were painted.*

suming the office, he proposed, and the Congress passed, a flurry of legislation setting up new agencies and programs, with units to administer them.

Among the most important of the new agencies was the Civilian Conservation Corps, which sent unemployed young men into camps throughout the United States to perform jobs of public works. A representative was chosen from each of four departments of the federal government. War set up the camps and furnished food, clothes, and semimilitary discipline. Labor selected the participants. Agriculture and Interior developed projects for the CCC boys. On the planning board

I represented Ickes for the Interior. It was an enormous job, but, incredibly, we filled our quota of 200,000 men in 200 camps throughout the country by June 1933—just a little over two months after Congress had set up the system. Along with this assignment Secretary Ickes directed the Public Works Administration (PWA), which placed additional responsiblity on the Park Service.

During the spring of 1933 I made my final decision to resign from government service, and I accepted a position with a company based in New York. I timed my resignation for August 10, 1933, the date of the implementation of the Reorganization Act, which increased the number of Park Service units from 63 to 128. I felt I had accomplished most of my goals for the National Park Service: helping bring it into existence; setting up the administrative structure and various divisions that were now well established; and finally drawing in the historic areas to be saved, along with the scenic ones.

The National Park Service had been established as a conservation and preservation organization. There was no question in my mind as to who should succeed me as director: Arno Cammerer. He was the most qualified—a trained and dedicated partner of Mather's and mine. It wasn't all that easy though, for Ickes, who liked relatively few people, had taken a dislike to him. The Secretary appointed a committee to choose a successor to me, and its first choice was Newton Drury, head of the Save-the-Redwoods League and a classmate of mine from the University of California. At this time he declined the offer, although he did accept after the breakdown of Cammerer's health in 1940.

When the amount of work Cammerer undertook and the stress he was under are considered, it is a wonder that he did not collapse sooner. There was probably no time since the early days

MARK GIBSON

THE WASHINGTON MONUMENT, Washington, D.C. *Built to honor George Washington, the famous landmark rises 555 feet above the city.*

DAVID MUENCH

THE LINCOLN MEMORIAL, Washington, D.C. *Inspirational in its marble setting, it imparts a sense of quiet and dignity. Completed in 1922, the memorial honors a president whose courage and vision are known throughout the world.*

Some of our country's most revered shrines are located in the city of Washington, D.C. The National Park Service has been accorded the honor of administering and preserving them for the thousands who come each year to view and receive inspiration from their nation's finest memorials.

VICKSBURG NATIONAL MILITARY PARK, Miss. *In 1862 an attempt by Union forces to gain undisputed control of the Mississippi River failed when a naval task force, spearheaded by the ironclad gunboat* Cairo, *was repulsed north of Vicksburg. The* Cairo *was sunk by electrically detonated mines. More than 100 years later the gunboat was raised from the river bottom and put on display in the USS* Cairo *Museum adjacent to the Vicksburg National Cemetery.*

of the Park Service that so many changes and so many burdens had been laid on a director. "Cam" was a loyal and compassionate man. He pushed hard for higher Civil Service classifications for his employees, both in Washington and in the field. His deep interest in advancing the participation of women in the Service resulted in a large increase in their numbers during his administration.

Now being emphasized were the social values and economic importance of park areas. The bureau found itself face to face with ideas for multiple land use. Preservation of natural resources gained momentum as people realized that these resources were finite and, once destroyed, could not be replaced. Thus new categories of park areas

GETTYSBURG NATIONAL MILITARY PARK, Pa.
For two days Union forces fought to contain the attack of the Army of Northern Virginia under the command of Confederate General Robert E. Lee. On the third day a bloody decision was reached, forcing the withdrawal of Lee's forces and leaving thousands dead and wounded on both sides. A monument to General Lee, astride his famous horse Traveler, marks the site of the battle.

FORD'S THEATRE NATIONAL HISTORIC SITE, Washington, D.C. *While attending the play* Our American Cousin *on April 14, 1865, President Lincoln was shot by actor John Wilkes Booth, who immediately leaped from the President's box to the stage and escaped. Lincoln died the following day. The theater, now carefully restored and maintained, houses many historic relics of Lincoln's life and of the events that took place on that tragic night.*

PAT JOHNSON

Throughout the national park system are many structures of historic importance that must be protected. They include individual houses, military forts, early trading posts, pioneer homes, and other sites. These may be restored to their original appearance or maintained against further deterioration.

were introduced, such as national seashores and national recreations areas.

This was only one side of the coin, however. Cammerer had inherited the projects of the CCC and PWA. The latter was changed to the Works Progress Administration (WPA). Other New Deal emergency-welfare ideas were introduced with what seemed to the National Park Service to be incredible amounts of money appropriated to carry them out. Add $216 million for federal works projects to the regular National Park Service appropriations, which climbed rapidly with each year until World War II, compare them with

DAVID MUENCH

MANASSAS NATIONAL BATTLEFIELD PARK, Va. *The pleasant rolling hills and grassy meadows surrounding a stone-built tavern furnished the locale for the first land battle of the Civil War. It was here the First Battle of Manassas took place on July 21, 1861. The old tavern quickly became a field hospital to treat the wounded. Known today as the Stone House, it has been restored to resemble a hospital of the Civil War period.*

Men of Vision—these are the people who "see" into the future. At Gettysburg, leaders on both sides fought to uphold what each thought was right for this nation. When he went to Washington, D.C., in the early 1900s, Horace Albright did not envision a great national park system, but he did see one evolving. To him the National Park Service became a true system only after the passage of the Government Reorganization Act of 1933.

a 1929 total of only $8,750,000, and you can see the enormous change in just a few years. Meticulous planning and precise execution of policies were required, and all administrative details had to be handled differently.

Fortunately Cammerer was helped by new personnel entering the Park Service. Because of the Depression, many outstanding, well-educated people went into government service. Because it expanded so rapidly, Cammerer could no longer oversee the entire park system from Washington. He established four regional administrative offices: east of the Mississippi, the Plains to the summit of the Rockies, the Southwest to the Mississippi, and the Rockies to the Pacific, including Alaska and Hawaii.

With the passage of the Historic Sites Act in 1935, Cammerer instituted a separate branch with

an assistant director at its head to administer just that type of area. He also added certain parks that had already been authorized in the administrations of previous directors, and he worked unceasingly to round out new ones, such as Olympic, Kings Canyon, Big Bend, and Everglades.

In 1939 Cammerer suffered a heart attack and never really regained his health. With an ever-increasing work load and the unreasoning enmity of the bad-tempered Ickes, Cam's many friends, as well as his doctors, urged him to step down to save his life. After careful examination and with deep regret, but with his usual grace, he resigned in June 1940 to become a regional director in Richmond, Virginia. Newton Drury replaced him as director. Cammerer lived less than a year. With him ended "the founding years" of the National Park Service.

Upon resigning, Albright wrote one of his most profound and eloquent statement
The original, intended only for his staff, was handwritten on sheets of pape
Fortunately, the pages were preserved by his daughter, Marian Schenc
This statement is just as true, dynamic, and challenging today as when it was written in 193.

K. C. DENDOOVEN, PUBLISH

STATEMENT BY HORACE M. ALBRIGHT
TO THE
NATIONAL PARK SERVICE PERSONNEL
UPON HIS RESIGNATION AS DIRECTOR IN 1933

In this letter, perhaps one of my last official statements to you, let me urge you to be aggressive and vigorous in the fulfillment of your administrative duties. The National Park Service, from its beginning, has been an outstanding organization because its leaders, both in Washington and out in the field, worked increasingly and with high public spirit to carry out the noble policies and maintain the lofty ideals of the service as expressed in law and executive pronouncement. Do not let the service become "just another Government bureau"; keep it youthful, vigorous, clean and strong. We are not here to simply protect what we have been given so far; we are here to try to be the future guardians of those areas as well as to sweep our protective arms around the vast lands which may well need us as man and his industrial world expand and encroach on the last bastions of wilderness. Today we are concerned about our natural areas being enjoyed for the people. But we must never forget that all the elements of nature, the rivers, forests, animals and all things co-existent with them must survive as well.

I hope that particular attention will be accorded always to that mandate in the National Park Service Act of 1916 and in many organic acts of the individual parks which enjoins us to keep our great parks in their natural condition. Oppose with all your strength and power all proposals to penetrate your wilderness regions with motorways and other symbols of modern mechanization. Keep large sections of primitive country free from the influence of destructive civilization. Keep these bits of primitive America for those who seek peace and rest in the silent places; keep them for the hardy climbers of the crags and peaks; keep them for the horseman and the pack train; keep them for the scientist and student of nature; keep them for all who would use their minds and hearts to know what God had created. Remember, once opened, they can never be wholly restored to primeval charm and grandeur.

I also urge you to be ever on the alert to detect and defeat attempts to exploit commercially the resources of the national parks. Often projects will be formulated and come to you "sugar-coated" with an alluring argument that the park will be benefited by its adoption. We National Park men and women know that nature's work as expressed in the world-famous regions in our charge cannot be improved upon by man.

Beware, too, of innovation in making the parks accessible. For a half century, elevators, cableways, electric railways and similar contrivances have been proposed from time to time and have been uniformly rejected. The airplane while now an excepted means of transportation should not be permitted to land in our primitive areas.

Park usefulness and popularity should not be measured in terms of mere numbers of visitors. Some precious park areas can easily be destroyed by the concentration of too many visitors. We should be interested in the quality of park patronage, not by the quantity. The parks, while theoretically are for everyone to use and enjoy, should be so managed that only those numbers of visitors that can enjoy them while at the same time not overuse and harm them would be admitted at a given time. We must keep elements of our crowded civilization to a minimum in our parks. Certain comforts, such as safe roads, sanitary facilities, water, food and modest lodging, should be available. Also extra care must be taken for the children, the elderly and the incapacitated to enjoy the beauty of the parks.

We have been compared to the military forces because of our dedication and esprit de corps. In a sense this is true. We do act as guardians of our country's land. Our National Park Service uniform which we wear with pride does command the respect of our fellow citizens. We have the spirit of fighters, not as a destructive force, but as a power for good. With this spirit each of us is an integral part of the preservation of the magnificent heritage we have been given, so that centuries from now people of our world, or perhaps of other worlds, may see and understand what is unique to our earth, never changing, eternal.

Horace M. Albright

The Idea Continues

Russ Dickenson started in a single-purpose job at Grand Canyon, the best known of all national parks. Like Horace Albright, he did not, could not, envision then the full scope of what the National Park System would become. World War II had just ended, the park service was expanding, the future held great promise.

Forty years ago, in 1946, I began work as a park ranger at Grand Canyon National Park. My interest in national parks had been whetted initially in a college geology class. Now that I look back on it, I find it remarkable that the National Park Service as an organization was only 30 years old then, though at the time, that was not important to me.

From the outset, I was struck by the plain old-fashioned wisdom of saving the best of America's natural and historical heritage for public enjoyment and enlightenment—now and for the future. I was glad to be a part of that. I have always been impressed by the unity of purpose, the dedication, commitment to principle, and camaraderie of National Park Service employees.

During the four years of World War II, the national parks had been virtually mothballed. There was little public use by visitors because of gas

GRAND CANYON NATIONAL PARK, Ariz. *The Canyon is eons of time sealed in stone, a natural museum of ancient life, an awesome example of what the forces of erosion can produce, and where the onlooker can experience a sense of spirituality. Even though these values were recognized, it took farsighted men to make the park possible. As far back as 1882 a bill to make Grand Canyon a national park was introduced to Congress. The bill failed to pass. In 1893 President Harrison designated the area as a forest preserve. President Theodore Roosevelt established it as a game preserve in 1906. In 1908 he designated it as a national monument. The Canyon was finally given national park status by Congress in 1918. It had taken 36 years to accomplish this result!*

GARY LADD

EL MORRO NATIONAL MONUMENT, N.Mex. *History carved in stone is an apt description of the inscriptions on the massive sandstone formation called El Morro by t. early Spanish conquistadores They first explored the area in 1605 and left inscriptions on t. rock walls telling of their visita tion. Their carvings were not t first. Like a historic register, th walls also bear the inscription: of Zuñi Indians, emigrants, traders, soldiers, Indian agent. and settlers. These inscription are protected against deface- ment or other damage.*

DAVID MUENCH

rationing and other constraints. Reduced crews of park rangers and other personnel performed nobly, protecting forest areas, wildlife, public buildings, and historic properties. With so little manpower available, fighting forest fires was a special concern. As funds were minimal for sal- aries and park operations, so was maintenance of buildings and facilities.

Then came the summer of 1946, the first travel season after World War II, and the American peo- ple hit the road! It was as if the tension on a spring had suddenly been released. They came by car, bus, and train, but mostly in the family automo- bile. Levels of visitation were unprecedented, and with inadequate work forces and facilities the parks strained to furnish a quality experience. In many instances, campgrounds and other accom- modations were completely overwhelmed. This situation arose despite the fact that the decade of the 1930s was one of the greatest periods of con- struction and facilities improvement in the his- tory of the Service.

Horace Albright, in the waning days of his directorship in the early 1930s, had sought and had obtained a leadership role for the National Park Service in Depression-era public works proj- ects. Director Arno Cammerer, who succeeded Albright, further promoted park activities for the evolving Civilian Conservation Corps.

Conrad L. Wirth, later a director of NPS, was at that time an assistant in Washington. At the outset he supervised and coordinated CCC work on state, county, and municipal parks, and sub- sequently, on all CCC projects in national parks.

MESA VERDE NATIONAL PARK, Colo. *Spectacular remains of an ancient Indian culture remain in the sheltered recesses of canyon walls in various parts of the park. Called the Anasazi, "the ancient ones," they lived and flourished in their stone cities for over 700 years before disappearing about A.D. 1200, leaving only traces behind that tell their story.*

GARY LADD

The CCC built or improved roads, trails, campgrounds, utility systems, restrooms, administration buildings, residences, and other facilities. Forestry activities such as reforestation, fire fighting, and cleanup were emphasized. The CCC accomplishments were impressive and long lasting. Their skills and handiwork remain on view today in most national and state parks of that era.

Park facilities were designed for a much lesser volume of public use than that of 1946 and following years. This is not to say that people were unhappy with their park experiences. On the contrary, most were very impressed by the extraordinary scenery of rugged mountains, deep canyons, lakes, rivers, varied wildlife, and wilderness characteristics found in most national parks.

People talked about their trips, showed pictures to friends and family, and influenced others to spend their annual vacations seeing Yellowstone, Yosemite, Grand Canyon, and all the other great national parks in the system. The Indian ruins and historical and other cultural units within the national park system also received increased usage. The parks were now popular destination objectives, and America's love affair with the national parks was well underway.

Newton Drury, a Californian and a renowned conservationist with a fine record of earlier work in saving the redwoods, was director of the National Park Service throught the decade of the 1940s. I recall having seen and listened to him at a superintendents' conference held at Grand Can-

DAVID MUENCH

HOPEWELL VILLAGE NATIONAL HISTORIC SITE, Pa. *Life in the village was dominated by the constant roar from the massive iron furnace and the red glow that blanketed the town at night. Such was the day-and-night experience of Hopewell Village during the years 1820–1840. The picturesque village has been restored as closely as possible to its original appearance.*

Overleaf: ORGAN PIPE CACTUS NATIONAL MONUMENT, Ariz. *The monument is a living desert museum displayed against a scenic backdrop furnished by the Ajo and the Puerto Blanco mountains. The organ pipe cactus, rare in the United States, shares its domain with such showy cousins as the saguaro, prickly pear, and chain-fruit cholla. On display is a wide assortment of mammals, birds, and reptiles that are well adapted to arid desert life. Photo by David Muench.*

MOUND CITY GROUP NATIONAL MONUMENT, Ohio. *The Indians who built the intriguing mounds are known only as the Hopewell people. Archaeological excavations indicate that between A.D. 200 and A.D. 500 they built villages along nearby river valleys. They hunted, fished, grew some crops, and constructed a network of burial mounds. These demonstrated the existence of a system of social rankings in the villages. What happened to these people is not known. The mounds experienced some damage through the years, but restoration work has largely repaired the problem.*

DAVID MUENCH

Flowing water has always been a source of enjoyment to people. National rivers and wild and scenic riverways offer opportunities to experience firsthand all the many aspects of stream communities. These include outstanding scenery, natural history, and recreational possibilities —all very attractive to those who enjoy canoeing, camping, and other outdoor activities.

OZARK NATIONAL SCENIC RIVERWAYS, Mo.
Two rivers, the Current and the Jacks Fork, flow through a region of exceptionally scenic and recreational values, giving the visitor a sense of closeness to the natural world.

yon in 1949. This meeting was attended by NPS superintendents, regional directors, and Director Drury and principal members of his Washington, D.C., staff.

Distinguished in appearance, experienced and articulate, Drury led discussions primarily focused on the continuing shortfall in funding for operating the parks at a satisfactory level and on the need for more facilities to serve the ever-increasing number of visitors. He also spoke on the necessity for museum and exhibit improvement and for more and better interpretive programs such as campfire programs, slide talks, and guided trail walks. I guess nothing really ever changes. As director 36 years later, I heard the same thing!

During World War II, Director Drury had his administrative and political skills thoroughly tested. One of the federal offices removed from the capital was that of the National Park Service. Drury and the headquarters staff set up in Chicago for the duration. They were separated from the usual congressional and secretarial relationships, thus creating a difficult period for both Drury and the Park Service.

Drury steadfastly resisted appeals for timber cutting, grazing, and other inappropriate uses of parks. One of those was the wartime demand for timber from Olympic National Park for use in aircraft construction. Drury masterfully maneuvered the cutters onto alternate sites not involving national parks. Olympic's old-growth western redcedar forest, unexcelled elsewhere in the world, was saved.

In the late 1940s a proposal to construct two dams within Dinosaur National Monument on the Green and Yampa rivers, both tributaries to the Colorado River, had been advanced by the Bureau of Reclamation. Drury was adamant. No

CANYON DE CHELLY NATIONAL MONUMENT, Ariz.
History lives along the river and in the canyon walls, and imagination takes one back hundreds of years to a time when early Puebloans inhabited the region. There were villages along the river and stone buildings in recesses in the canyon walls and perched on high ledges. The Puebloans departed long ago, and Navajos now occupy and farm the valley, but the original scene remains the same.

dams were to be built in national parks. The mistake earlier in the century of permitting construction of the Hetch Hetchy dam at Yosemite was recalled.

Those of us working in parks at the time admired the courage and forthrightness of Newton Drury and of other individuals and organizations in resisting the dams. Political pressures associated with the Echo Park dam site in Dinosaur ultimately led to Drury's resignation. He refused to compromise the basic principles associated with protection of wild and scenic areas. I have always remembered this.

When I was starting out with the Service, I was fortunate to get to know a few of the park superintendents and other administrators who possessed a distinct character, aura, and forthrightness. Many were "Mather Men." Of those whom I recall most vividly, a special word.

Dr. Harold Bryant, superintendent of Grand Canyon from 1940 to 1954. He was one of the founders of the NPS interpretive programs, dating back into the 1920s, and served as NPS chief of interpretation in Washington, D.C., in the 1930s.
"White Mountain" Smith, longtime superintendent of Zion National Park.
Tom Allen, Tom Vint, John Coffman, Evind Scoyen, Herb Evison, Isabelle Story, Hillory Tolson, Jess Nusbaum, Miner Tillotson, P. P. Patraw, Hugh Miller, Jack Emmert—and the roll call could go on and on.

They, and hundreds unnamed, served with courage and perseverance as superintendents, rangers, foresters, landscape architects, engineers, historians, archeologists, and writer/editors. The common trait among all of these uncommon people, however, was their dedication to the national parks and the National Park Service, and they demonstrated that with lasting effect.

During my six years at Grand Canyon National Park, I was stationed at various times on both the North and South rims, rode horseback on Inner Canyon patrol for two summers, and did all the usual ranger duties: fire fighting, search and rescue, hunting-season boundary patrol, entrance-station operation, and information service for arriving visitors. We were a small group. There were only ten permanent rangers for the entire park.

Meeting the Santa Fe Railroad's daily passenger train from Williams, Arizona, to the Grand Canyon was one of the highly coveted duties. The more senior rangers had priority, but I won the assignment occasionally. The distinctive park-

ALLEN HAGOOD

DINOSAUR NATIONAL MONUMENT, Colo.-Utah.
Rivers have played a lead role in producing the story of the monument. Preserved in the sands of an ancient river, and now exposed at Dinosaur Quarry, are the bones of such giants as Brontosaurus and Allosaurus, relics of the Age of Reptiles. Providing a spectacular setting are the canyons carved by a great river, the Green. One river finished its work; the other is still active.

ranger uniform was highly respected by visitors and drew them like a magnet for questions, to "take a picture of the ranger," or for just plain conversation. Many liked to be reassured about the unfamiliar setting and circumstances.

Those park rangers who are truly successful have a common trait—one that does not show on their diploma. They like people and want to share with them knowledge of the parks and their natural history and the enjoyment and satisfaction to be gained from their use. Rangers inform the unwary of dangers and pitfalls and assist if trouble strikes. Every successful park ranger possesses this quality: a commitment to assist and

WHISKEYTOWN-SHASTA-TRINITY NATIONAL RECREATION AREA, Calif. *If the surrounding mountains could speak, they would give fascinating accounts of events and places now covered by Whiskeytown, Shasta, and Trinity lakes. Some are about Wintu-speaking Indians; some concern famous scout Jedediah Smith; and some are of the gold rush of 1848 and the subsequent birth of nearby mining towns. Today boaters, fishermen, and bathers, mostly unaware of what lies beneath, enjoy the quiet waters of these lakes.*

LAKE MEAD NATIONAL RECREATION AREA, Ariz.-Nev. *Desert and water, mountains and canyons combine to make this, the first national recreation area in the nation, a favorite vacationland for millions of people. In so doing, it provides excellent fishing, boating, water skiing, sailing, camping, exploring, nature study, Indian lore, and river history. A once hostile-appearing desert landscape has been permanently altered.*

help the public. That factor, I think, has been an important asset in building the broad base of public support existing today for national parks.

When I began, ranger training was done on a park-by-park basis, if at all, and mostly on the job. More experienced rangers would generally explain or demonstrate procedures to the novice.

One or two exceptions existed. Annual forest-fire training was well organized on both local and regional levels. An annual two-week training course emphasizing policy, management, and administration for promising, promotable employees was led by Assistant Director Hillory Tolson. This course was familiarly known as "Tolson Tech." It was the forerunner of the Service's outstanding ranger training program now located at the Albright Training Center at Grand Canyon and the Mather Training Center, Harpers Ferry, West Virginia. The Service also participates in the Federal Law Enforcement Training Center in Glynnco, Georgia.

The Service's first training officer was Park Ranger Frank Kowski who had developed Yellowstone's program. Talented, personable, and aggressive, he was transferred to Washington in 1951 to set up a servicewide training program. A lesser spirit would have failed, but Frank became a legend. From his efforts grew "Kowski Kollege," a broad-based orientation and operations course

CAPE COD NATIONAL SEASHORE, Mass. *Mention of a seashore usually brings to mind such things as swimming, sunbathing, surf fishing, sea life, nature walks, sand dunes, and long views along the ocean front. One also gets a feel of the nation's history in the Provincetown area, where the Pilgrims first landed in 1620. The Cape also has other historic sites.*

PADRE ISLAND NATIONAL SEASHORE, Tex. *A clean, undeveloped beach stretches for more than 80 miles along the Texas Gulf Coast, and along its length Nature offers a wide assortment of sea and land life. More than 350 species of birds and several kinds of mammals and reptiles are year-round residents or seasonal visitors. Recreational opportunities are many and varied.*

established at Yosemite, then moved permanently to quarters at Grand Canyon and named the Albright Training Center. Frank Kowski was later an admired and respected superintendent and regional director.

By the time Conrad L. Wirth became director in the early 1950s, the imbalance between demand and supply in the national park system had reached serious proportions. In the field we tried to make do with what we had. Common practice was to provide overflow campgrounds and to put patch on top of patches. We needed more of everything to deal with the flood of visitors.

Employee housing was, in many cases, deplorable and in short supply everywhere. The impact of visitor use and the need to recover from years of meager appropriations were being recognized by the media, Congress, and the general public.

Years later, after I had become director, Connie

Wirth told me that his concern had been how to present the needs of the Service in a way that would overcome the limitations and problems of year-to-year funding. He said that early in 1955 he had spent a weedend thinking of a strategy for a multiyear approach and did some estimating of dollar requirements and number of years to accomplish specific goals. The completion date would be ten years hence, on the fiftieth anniversary of the NPS. Out of his concern came a solution and the appropriate name: "Mission 66." He presented the concept at a staff meeting on the following Monday. It was enthusiastically received, and so the process of approval began.

WAR IN THE PACIFIC NATIONAL HISTORICAL PARK, Guam. *The high point of Nimitz Hill looks down upon the "blue" and "green" sectors of Asan Beach and Asan Point, twin objectives of the U.S. Marine offensive that stormed ashore on Guam in 1944. The park is comprised of seven detached units. They feature various aspects of the battle for possession of the island and include many historic objects such as gun emplacements, pillboxes, caves, and foxholes.*

The turning point came when President Dwight Eisenhower invited Wirth to explain the proposed revitalization of the national parks at a Cabinet meeting at the White House. The President approved, and later congressional briefings and committee hearings were equally supportive. In 1955 I was the superintendent of Chiricahua National Monument, scenic mountain-and-canyon country located north of Douglas, Arizona. This was the land of Cochise, where the Chiricahua Apaches had made a last stand in the late 1800s. Imagine my delight and that of my colleagues when Director Wirth announced Mission 66, a ten-year program to bring every park up to a satisfactory standard. From every area of the system plans and funding requests flowed in for road repairs, visitor centers, employee housing, bridges, trails, and water and sewer systems.

I recall the long hours and the extensive paper work involved in preparing plans for Chiricahua—modest in comparison to complex areas like Grand Canyon or Yellowstone. I transferred before any Mission 66 projects were approved for Chiricahua,

CHANNEL ISLANDS NATIONAL PARK, Calif. *Where the mountains meet the sea is the essence of these island seascapes. Booming waves as they crash against the cliff, tidewater pools teeming with life, pelicans nesting on the slopes, sea lions sunning themselves on the rocks, and a refreshing breath of sea air—these are the special gifts of the Channel Islands.*

but I did have the satisfaction years later of returning to see the fine results of the 1955 plans.

As usual, there were critics who thought the parks were being overdeveloped. But there were even more who deplored the inadequate facilities and deteriorating conditions at the parks. From my vantage point in the field, then and later, I believed that the parks would have been sorely damaged without a Mission 66, and the American public would not have been well served.

Originally it had been planned to have the parks handle 80 million visitors by 1966, a poor estimate as it turned out. The number of visitors by that year was actually 133 million. During this ten-year period, new parks were added, new plans were made, and funding was adjusted. The amount expended for improvements in Mission 66 was about $1 billion. Quite simply, Mission 66 has to rank as one of the greatest aids to visitor service and long-range protection from overuse and abuse in the history of the Service.

When I was chief ranger of Grand Teton National Park for the five-year period from 1957 to 1962, I observed firsthand some results of Mission 66. For instance, the scenic, more convenient bypass road from Moose to Moran, Wyoming, was built, relieving pressure on the sensitive Jenny Lake region. An entirely new headquarters/administrative complex was constructed at Moose, which is more accessible and farther away from the base of the Tetons. And the new public-use area at Colter Bay increased overall visitor-use

DAVID MUENCH

EISENHOWER NATIONAL HISTORIC SITE, Pa.
The strength and the character shown by this president during his lifetime of service are reflected in his home. Situated in a countryside setting, the house offers calm, peace, and quiet beauty. Once a 200-year-old log cabin, the house had to be completely redesigned and rebuilt as Mamie and he visualized it.

capacity and dispersed that usage to the north end of Jackson Lake and the park.

Many other public-use and park-protection projects were completed—far too many to list. But Grand Teton was one park of many that could not have survived without Mission 66.

PETER FRENCH

USS *ARIZONA* MEMORIAL, Hawaii. *Looking into the clear waters of Pearl Harbor, where the battleship USS* Arizona *rests on the bottom, one experiences a sense of loss and sadness that does not easily pass. As a memorial, a viewing and exhibit structure rises above the sunken ship to aid visitors to understand the events that took place. A wall exhibit lists the names of all the men who lie permanently entombed.*

GULF ISLANDS NATIONAL SEASHORE, Fla.-Miss.
Miles of white sand beaches bordered by windblown dunes form the seaward sides of the barrier islands for which the area is famous. Sea oats strive valiantly to hold the dunes in place with their elaborate, effective stem and root systems. Behind the dunes is a different world of shrubs, trees, and coastal marshes.

DAVID MUENCH

With interest in conservation growing, park visitation rising, and increasing population and urban growth, many conservationists believed that an obvious strategy was to add more parks. Potential parks and worthy historic sites were being lost to competitive uses, they felt. The opportunity to "round out" the national park system would occur in the two decades from 1960 to 1980.

An important survey of the nation's seashores and the Great Lakes yielded only a few remaining park-system candidates to add to Cape Hatteras, North Carolina, the first national seashore, authorized in 1937. Those identified as having the requisite characteristics are outstanding indeed:

North Carolina's Cape Lookout, Cape Cod in Massachusetts, Assateague Island along Maryland and Virginia, Wisconsin's Apostle Islands, Cumberland Island off the coast of Georgia, Gulf Islands along Florida and Mississippi, and Michigan's Pictured Rocks and Sleeping Bear Dunes.

George B. Hartzog, Jr., became director in 1964. With his combination of Washington and field expertise and the tenor of the times, NPS experienced one of its greatest growth periods. In the nine years of Director Hartzog's leadership, NPS aggressively carried out a new-areas study program. Its goal was to bring outstanding and nationally significant park areas into the system while they were available and undamaged.

Altogether, about 100 new areas were added to the system by Congress, bringing the total to 297 in 1972. How fortunate we are today to have national parks like Redwood in California, Washington State's North Cascades, Virgin Islands, Voyageurs in Minnesota, and Florida's Biscayne Bay; and Longfellow National Historic Site in Massachusetts and the Chesapeake and Ohio Canal National Historical Park along the Potomac River. This incorporation of new units into the national park system was a brilliant accomplish-

DAVID MUENCH

CANAVERAL NATIONAL SEASHORE, Fla.
Pummeled by ocean waves on one side and soothed by quietly lapping waters of Mosquito Lagoon on the other, this barrier island is in constant physical change. It is home to such unusual animals as the ghost crab, the sea turtle, and the manatee. Black Point Wildlife Drive offers an excellent place to observe marsh and wading birds and waterfowl.

CAPE HATTERAS NATIONAL SEASHORE, N.C. *For ages a contest between wind, sea, and sand has been fought along the Outer Banks, a string of barrier islands separating the surf of the Atlantic from the calmer waters toward the mainland. The area is excellent for bird watching, as several freshwater and saltwater ponds and marshes attract both resident and migratory species. Here also there are three lighthouses, the Cape Hatteras Lighthouse being the tallest in North America.*

ment, one for which the American people should be forever grateful. If it had not happened then, many sites would have been lost forever.

These two decades of dramatic expansion brought a heightened clash of values, however. Establishment of new parks involved purchases of privately owned property—homes, businesses, lots, farms, and ranches. In some instances resistance was very real. Costs were high in dollars and also in relationships with nearby communities and park neighbors. Concern was expressed that the selection process not be politicized and that the integrity and special quality of NPS areas not be compromised. Congress authorizes new areas for addition to the system, but the National Park Service takes the brunt of the opposition.

INDIANA DUNES NATIONAL LAKESHORE, Ind. *Sand dunes, especially large ones, have always been a favorite with those who enjoy the outdoors. Dunes in this area are constantly on the move. A large dune one day may be much reduced by wind a week later. Neighboring ponds, bogs, and wooded areas attract wildlife.*

VOYAGEURS NATIONAL PARK, Minn. *Glaciers, some more than a mile thick, ground their way through the area at least four times in the last million years. They scoured out shallow basins and left behind more than 30 lakes that now form the heart of the park. Surrounding forests are the homes of abundant wildlife, including wolves and bears.*

JEFF GNASS

During 1963–1964, I was an assistant superintendent at Zion National Park, Utah, then superintendent in 1965–1966 of the Flaming Gorge National Recreation Area in Utah. The former is an old-time national park; the latter is a recreational area and a newcomer to the system. Their differences are pronounced, and many NPS employees have experienced these contrasts as the Service expanded to administer national recreation areas, seashores, and historic sites, in addition to national parks and monuments. Different policies, different problems, different solutions.

Changes were occurring in many ways. The public was becoming much more environmentally aware. Congress responded during the 1960s with a spate of laws relating to outdoor recreation, wilderness, clean water and air, and protection of the environment. Protests against the war in Vietnam, disturbances in the cities, civil rights demonstrations—all had their impact on the NPS.

After spending 1967 as chief of New Area Studies and Master Planning in Washington, D.C., I moved across the Washington Channel to Headquarters, National Capital Parks, for five and a half years. During those years I witnessed hundreds of demonstrations—many large and sometimes violent—starting with Resurrection City. The U.S. Park Police and other officers, and occasionally the Army and National Guard, attempted to preserve order. It was a time of testing, a time of national crisis. Hundreds of thousands of people were involved. Protecting the constitutional right to exercise the freedoms granted by the First Amendment became for many of us practically a full-time occupation. Use of park lands for protest of grievances inevitably conflicted with their use for recreation and public pleasuring grounds.

To be more responsive to the changes occurring all around us, a new urban, community-oriented program was initiated. Summer in the Parks began in 1968 in Washington, D.C., on the Mall and other parklands administered by NPS in the District of Columbia. (About 20 percent of the District has been set aside as parklands.) This program featured educational and recreational activities, community involvement, arts and crafts, and entertainment—all family oriented. It succeeded in meeting the needs of those days. Its legacy is ongoing, and park and recreation activity programs today testify to its success and its lasting impact throughout the Service.

It was during this period also that the "living history" interpretive programs were developed. At many sites of historic significance NPS personnel wear period-style clothing and demonstrate

BRUCE NYDEN

VIRGIN ISLANDS NATIONAL PARK, St. John, V.I. *The name Virgin Islands conjures up visions of a tropical sea, balmy days on white sand beaches, and coral reefs of many colors. Also within this park are prehistoric Indian sites and artifacts and remains of Danish colonial sugar plantations. All of these features combine to make this area one of the most diverse in the national park system.*

BUCK ISLAND REEF NATIONAL MONUMENT, St. Croix, V.I. *An entirely new and exotic world lies hidden in the warm sea waters of this southeasternmost of national parks and monuments. A colorful assortment of tropical fishes inhabit the grottos and can be viewed during guided snorkeling tours or by using underwater self-guiding trails.*

MORRISTOWN NATIONAL HISTORICAL PARK, N.J. *A weary Continental Army under General Washington set up winter quarters at Morristown in 1777. They faced a desperate time when both shelter and food were scarce. Finding new recruits and maintaining a fighting force were difficult. Living history presentations now tell the story of those trying days in the life of our nation.*

many of the activities in which early residents engaged. Visitors gain keen insights into the daily life, challenges, and conditions faced by pioneer families.

The affection that Americans have for national parks and historic sites has never been more superbly demonstrated than during the one hundredth anniversary of Yellowstone National Park in 1972. Throughout the year there were special observances in Washington, D.C., and elsewhere. An early highlight was a television program from New York City featuring Director Hartzog, Horace Albright, and other notables. Another event was a banquet in Washington, D.C., attended by Cabinet officials and members of Congress.

As the world's first national park, Yellowstone attracted national and international attention that

FORT JEFFERSON NATIONAL MONUMENT, Fla.
A once strategic nineteenth-century American fort no longer serves in the defense of the country. Instead, it offers safe haven for a vast assortment of marine life. Multicolored animals of the coral reefs, huge sea turtles, and the nesting grounds for thousands of sooty terns help give the area its unique qualities.

WASHINGTON CAPITOL PARKS, D.C. *Like a banner flung across the land and inscribed with names of the Vietnam War dead, this massive granite wall is a special tribute to those who gave their life for their country. War memorials are often centered around a triumphant column or sculptured figures. This one is uniquely different. Each name, as on a great roll of honor, is individually presented for all the nation to see.*

year, culminating in a grand celebration at the famous Washburn-Langford-Doane campfire site in September. Featured speakers in an outstanding program were Mrs. Richard Nixon, representing the President, and Secretary of the Interior Rogers C. B. Morton. I shall never forget that program. A vivid memory remains of the President's wife, Secretary Morton, and other dignitaries sitting stoically on an uncovered speakers' platform, struggling to read speeches during an unexpected snowstorm.

But times were changing, and I experienced firsthand some of those changing times. Contrary to prior historical patterns and traditions, the NPS underwent several quick successions in leadership during the decade of the seventies, with four different directors. I was deputy director to two of those directors, Ron Walker and Gary Everhardt, for two and one-half years.

I was also fortunate to be in a position to add impetus to the Service's Bicentennial program. This involved bringing up to standard, with new or improved visitor centers and other important visitor facilities, about 25 units of the system that were associated with the Revolutionary War and the founding of the United States. Independence

FORT LARNED NATIONAL HISTORIC SITE, Kans.
This was the home of the famous Buffalo Soldiers, a unit of black soldiers that made up the fort's company during its heydey. Theirs was the task of furnishing protection for settlers pushing westward through Kansas. Today, living history demonstrations portray the experiences of these soldiers.

HOME OF FRANKLIN D. ROOSEVELT NATIONAL HISTORIC SITE, N.Y. *Springwood, the home in Hyde Park of the thirty-second president of the United States, is an excellent reflection of his character. It was at this house, overlooking a beautiful view of the Hudson River, that his political career began. It was here also that he made many historic decisions that were to affect the world.*

National Historical Park in Philadelphia was the focal point of our efforts, but we also devoted great energy to Yorktown, Virginia; Morristown, New Jersey; Minuteman, Massachusetts; Fort Mc-Henry, Maryland; and such lesser-known places as Cowpens, South Carolina, and Fort Stanwix, New York.

For the four years preceding 1976, the NPS budget had emphasized the buildup of Bicentennial areas. Thus the construction budget for those years was concentrated in the northeastern part of the country, to the consternation of superintendents and regional directors in the rest of the United States.

In my opinion, one of the success stories of NPS was its 1976 contributions to the two hundredth anniversary of the country's birth. Lasting improvements resulted: visitor centers, parking areas, roads, interpretive trails, restoration of historic structures—all aimed at better visitor understanding of historic events. Touring exhibits and interpretive programs touched most NPS areas throughout the country.

No one involved in the small, special Bicentennial action group will ever forget that period. We *made* things happen despite the vagaries of weather, contractors' schedules, and other "unsolvable" problems. The designated areas were ready by July 4, 1976, and Director Gary Everhardt proudly represented the Service and its achievements and contributions during the Bicentennial Year. Millions of Americans toured Revolutionary War and other sites associated with American independence that year. The July 4 event on the Mall in Washington, D.C., may never be surpassed.

The director of the National Park Service is not an elected official; he is appointed by the President and the Secretary of the Interior. Senate confirmation is not required. A director is expected to be experienced in park and recreation administration. He is also expected to understand and be a part of the political process, but not to be a politician in a partisan sense.

The rather rapid turnover in directors in the 1970s can only be viewed as part of a trend toward politicization of the Service. Further, Congress di-

LOWELL NATIONAL HISTORICAL PARK, Mass. *Quiet waters reflect the dream of John Cabot Lowell, who in 1822 designed and built the first cotton mill. One year later the mill produced its first manufactured cloth. The town was given the name of Lowell in 1836, making it our first planned, organized, and incorporated industrial city.*

BOSTON NATIONAL HISTORICAL PARK, Mass. *The year 1797 marked the building of what was to become the oldest comissioned warship in the world. She never lost a battle in her entire career and became famous as Old Ironsides. Today she is known as the USS Constitution.*

Throughout the country there are a number of features and buildings of historic importance that lack the qualifications for individual national designation. They are included in recreational areas and historical parks and are thus given protection and recognition.

DAVID MUENCH

rected that an annual list of 12 candidate areas for addition to the system be submitted for its consideration. With the increasingly attractive political and economic benefits associated with national park status, the result was a sizable increase in new areas authorized by Congress.

Although Congress makes the final determination of areas of national significance proposed for the park system, concern had been raised by NPS and other organizations and groups about the quality, integrity, and merit of some areas brought into the system in the 1970s. A sense of organizational unrest crept into the Service, administrative problems multiplied, and overall morale dropped. A clash between Director William Whalen and the Conference of National Park Concessioners led to his dismissal by Interior Secretary Cecil Andrus in the spring of 1980.

This was a particularly critical time, as governmentwide budgetary problems were seriously affecting the Park Service. It was certainly common knowledge within the Service that the rapid expansion of the system had been accomplished at the expense of existing older areas. A decrease in the number of personnel and a decline in the level and quality of service occurred at a time when visitors, management problems, and the number of parks were increasing.

SAN JUAN ISLAND NATIONAL HISTORICAL PARK, Wash. *A hungry British pig wandered into an American farmer's garden and proceeded to root it up, almost causing a war between English and American forces over who owned the island. Such was the Pig War of 1859. Fortunately the dispute was settled amicably, and in 1872 the United States acquired the entire island by treaty.*

CRATERS OF THE MOON NATIONAL MONUMENT, Idaho. *Desolation intensified, a land as devoid of life as a moonscape—these impressions permeate the bleak landscape. In the twisted and broken lava can be seen the story of an awesome force within the earth as it spewed out rivers of molten rock only a few thousand years ago. Scarcely noticed are the dozens of plants and animals that thrive within this area.*

Secretary Andrus made it known that he was seeking for NPS a director with wide experience in park administration who had the support of Service personnel as well as park interest groups— a true professional. Andrus wanted, in his own words, "an old pro," someone who could bolster morale and get the Service back on its feet. In a consensus, regional directors and other top managers in the system recommended me for the job. Of course, the Secretary sought advice from many other sources.

BERING LAND BRIDGE NATIONAL PRESERVE, Alaska. *More than 13,000 years ago a land bridge furnished a migration route for prehistoric hunters, animals, and plants entering North America from Asia. Time passed; the sea covered a portion of the land bridge. Only a remnant of the former bridge, now encompassed in NPS's northwesternmost unit, is left to tell the story.*

ALASKA. *It is aptly called The Great Land, for not only is Alaska one-fifth the size of the continental United States, but it also contains superlative examples of natural features, wild lands, and human history. In 1980 several of these areas were granted national park, national monument, or national preserve status. There are now 15 such units in the national park system.*

ALAN ROBINSON

OLYMPIC NATIONAL PARK, Wash. *Water, in its many aspects, constitutes the heart of this evergreen world. Moisture-laden sea winds sweep inland, nurturing magnificient rain forests and dropping rain and snow on the high peaks. Meltwater from the snow fields moves seaward, feeding numerous lakes, waterfalls, and rivers. Along the coast, pounding waves relentlessly tear away the shoreline.*

DAVID MUENCH

OLYMPIC NATIONAL PARK. *Undisturbed beaches, sea stacks, and inviting tidal pools offer a sense of solitude along the coastal portion of the park. It is in this picturesque setting that rivers such as the Quillayute, Queets, and Hoh meet the sea.*

CANYONLANDS NATIONAL PARK, Utah. *A wilderness in sandstone is the basic motif of this park. It is in the midst of a vast assortment of canyons, buttes, spires, and natural bridges that two giant rivers—the Colorado and the Green—meet to combine their canyon-cutting efforts. From the canyon rims a bewildering maze of rock formations stretches for miles, a giant jigsaw puzzle that only Nature could have fashioned.*

In April 1980 I had been Pacific Northwest regional director for over four years and had been giving special attention to studies on proposed new Alaskan parks when the Secretary asked for my thoughts on the director's job and NPS. "It is time for us to consolidate the gains that have been made," I told him. After he appointed me, that philosophy became the focus of my efforts during five years as director in both the Carter and

BLACK CANYON OF THE GUNNISON NATIONAL MONUMENT, Colo. *Gazing into the dark-walled canyon, one tends to alternate between appreciation of its beauty and cautious recognition of its depth and narrowness and of the sheerness of its walls. Even the clear stream far below has an unreal quality. Sunlight penetrates the canyon sparingly, adding to its somber mood.*

Reagan administrations. Neither Secretary Andrus nor subsequent secretaries Jim Watt, William Clark, or Don Hodel ever asked of me my political party affiliation or preference. I was there because of my experience and recognition as a career professional.

One of the outstanding conservation achievements of the twentieth century was the Alaska National Interest Lands Conservation Act, signed by President Jimmy Carter in December 1980. The completion of this long effort occurred while I was in office, though each director from George Hartzog on had worked toward this goal. Much credit for success must be accorded Secretary Andrus, Congressman Morris "Mo" Udall of Arizona, John Seiberling of Ohio, many other members of the Senate and House, and a coalition of national conservation organizations. I was present at the White House at the signing of the Alaska bill that brought into the system a dozen new wild and beautiful areas, more than doubling the total acreage of the national park system.

That was a proud moment, but the early years of overseeing these areas has been difficult. Opposition and lingering animosity remain among Alaskans toward the concept of national parks in

DEATH VALLEY NATIONAL MONUMENT, Calif. *Wind, the artist, while moving sand along the valley floor sometimes exposes intricately weathered rock, at the same time building gently curving dunes that cover large areas. For the past several thousand years this natural erosive force has done much to give the valley its present shape.*

their state, though these feelings now seem to be easing. Insufficient funds and personnel to properly survey, inventory, and protect invaluable wildlife and other wild resources compound the problem.

When the Republicans won the presidential election of November 1980, I fully expected to be replaced as director by a Republican appointee, probably from outside the career service staff. By January 1981 it was clear that James Watt would be nominated as Secretary of the Interior. He in turn asked me to continue as director. Every other Carter administration bureau chief in the Department of the Interior was replaced. I was the sole survivor. Secretary Watt also told me that his mission was to be a lightning rod for change and that he might have a relatively short tenure. This dis-

RAINBOW BRIDGE NATIONAL MONUMENT, Utah.
The Navajo Indians have a name for the world's largest natural bridge: Nonnezoshi, "rainbow in stone." They consider this bridge to be a sacred place. Although there are other natural bridges in the region, none have the graceful beauty of this sandstone giant.

MOUNT RUSHMORE NATIONAL MEMORIAL, S.Dak. *Chiseled into the face of a nearly indestructible 60-million-year-old granite mountain is the record of 150 years of American history. The carved heads of four presidents stand out in bold relief, symbolizing the ideals and trials at the time each was chief of state.*

Maintenance

The care of our national parks presents unique challenges. From rebuilding prehistoric Indian ruins to refurbishing the Statue of Liberty, specialized knowledge, skills, materials, and equipment are necessary.

In historic areas some artifacts and structures must be repaired or restored with the same techniques and tools that were used originally. At Mount Rushmore the annual inspection and cleaning is a job of derring-do that is not for the faint-hearted.

Truly, the special requirements of protection and perpetuation of the unequaled resources of our national parks make maintenance an invisible but vital element of the responsibilities of the National Park Service.

closure prompted me to set new priorities on what I was attempting to accomplish in behalf of the Service.

One of my first requests to the new secretary was a $100-million-per-year program for five years to correct health and safety problems in the parks. These problems, highlighted in a General Accounting Office report of October 1980, dealt with aging water, sewer, electrical systems, and with deteriorating buildings and roads. Health and environmental standards and safety codes had been raised in the 1960s and 1970s. However, the Service's budget had not always permitted remedial action, and growth and expansion had drained funds for possible improvements.

After a few days' study, Secretary Watt called me in and stated that he was appalled by the report. He thought my program ought to be increased to $200 million per year for five years—a $1-billion Park Restoration and Improvement Program! While not all of the $200 million proposed annually would be new or additional funding, a large proportion *would* be, particularly following the passage of a five-cent-a-gallon sales tax on gasoline to bolster the Federal Highway Trust Fund. Segments of the interstate highway system

STATUE OF LIBERTY NATIONAL MONUMENT, N.Y.-N.J. *"Give me your tired, your poor, your huddled masses yearning to breathe free," reads a portion of the inscription at this symbol of freedom. Come they did—by the thousands—to help form the foundation of our society. However, this inspiring gift from the people of France finally began to yield to the destructive forces of nature. The structure began to weaken; the metal parts corroded. The necessary refurbishment was done, and the project was completed in 1986 in time for the observance of Liberty's one hundredth year.*

MAMMOTH CAVE NATIONAL PARK, Ky. *The discovery of an opening into one of the world's largest caves was made by prehistoric Indians perhaps as long ago as 4,000 years. Imagination must have played a great role as, equipped with torches, they peered cautiously into the great rooms and passageways. Seeing the many beautiful stalagmite and stalactite formations, finding a river that ran underground, and even discovering a small lake must have seemed mysterious to them.*

DAVID MUENCH

badly needed repairs, but so did national park roads. Many parkways and park roads remained uncompleted. As passed by Congress, a small portion of the annual gas tax revenue received by NPS was applied to the Park Restoration and Improvement Program.

The Reagan administration and Congress, despite some partisan battling and bickering, basically agreed with the identified needs and the proposed funding levels. For five years, work was done on facilities supporting visitor activities and services in all parks, with emphasis on the older ones, to raise them to a higher standard. In my own mind I rank this achievement with those of the CCC and Mission 66. We would certainly have been in bad trouble without it. There is more to be done, particularly the drawing up and implementation of a stable, long-range program of cyclic maintenance.

My term as director was essentially one of "consolidating our gains," attempting to strengthen operations and visitor services, and dealing with environmental and developmental changes affecting every facet of the system. Attention was given to promoting natural- and cultural-area preservation. The response and support of the entire National Park Service is something I shall never forget.

DAVID MUENCH

WIND CAVE NATIONAL PARK, S.Dak. *A strong wind whistling from a small hole in the ground led to the discovery of this huge cavern. It was promptly named Wind Cave. It is the "boxwork," honeycomb-shaped structures of calcite in the walls and ceilings, that makes this cave unique. A second feature of exceptionally delicate beauty is nearby Jewel Cave National Monument.*

GOLDEN SPIKE NATIONAL HISTORIC SITE, Utah. *The word "done," flashed by telegraph from coast to coast, signaled the driving of the last spike in the building of America's first transcontinental railroad. Never again were West and East separated by vast distances and mountain barriers.*

GREAT BASIN NATIONAL PARK, Nev. *Leman Caves, formerly a national monument, offers a limestone fairyland of stalactites, stalagmites, and flowstone formations. Wheeler Peak rises 13,061 feet above the Snake Range, making it the second highest mountain in the state. Glaciers sculpted the mountain's rugged highlands and lake basins. Extensive forests reach a climax with exceptional stands of the world's oldest trees, the bristlecone pines. Great Basin, the newest of our national parks, was established in 1986.*

ISLE ROYALE NATIONAL PARK, Mich. *There is a feel of wilderness about the island, and on every hand there are evidences that such is true. Miles of unspoiled forest and numerous undisturbed lakes help to create a feeling of solitude. Often the calm is broken by the howl of a wolf or the movement of a moose along a lakeshore.*

GEORGE WASHINGTON CARVER NATIONAL MONUMENT, Mo. *"It is simply service that measures success." These words were the guide to Carver's work and the principle by which he lived. As an educator, botanist, and agronomist he was a model after whom many young blacks could set standards. As a scientist he developed the lowly peanut and the sweet potato into an array of products.*

SAINT-GAUDENS NATIONAL HISTORIC SITE, N.H. *It was the artistic genius in Augustus Saint-Gaudens that created the buildings and grounds at the home where he spent much of his life. An important part of the landscaping was a formal garden of exceptional beauty. It was here he achieved fame as a sculptor, producing such masterpieces as the "Standing Lincoln" and "Diana."*

BOOKER T. WASHINGTON NATIONAL MONUMENT, Va. *The log cabin where he was born a slave represents more than just the birthplace of Booker T. Washington. It is symbolic of his life, the hardships he encountered, and his success in overcoming them. Like this sturdy cabin, his legacy of achievement has endured and is particularly evident in the field of education through the Tuskegee Institute, which he founded.*

TOM TILL

JEFF GNASS

MOUNT RAINIER NATIONAL PARK, Wash.
Glaciers, reaching 27 icy fingers down the sides of the mountain, show in vivid detail the eternal struggle that exists between two of Nature's greatest forces: the volcanic force that produced the great peak and the relentless power of ice tearing it asunder. There is a majestic beauty about the snow-clad peak that is enhanced by magnificent flower fields and forests. Indians regarded the mountain with awe tinged with fear.

ROCKY MOUNTAIN NATIONAL PARK, Colo. *With over one third of the park made up of snow-mantled peaks and tundra, this is truly high-country wilderness. Spread across the tundra are fields of flowers that contain many plants characteristic of the Arctic. In the lower elevations the wilderness changes to glacier-formed lakes, heavy forest, and valley meadows replete with flowers. Many kinds of wildlife round out the scene.*

GLEN CANYON NATIONAL RECREATIO
AREA, Utah-Ariz. *This mile-long man-mad lake provides boating, fishing, and gene relaxation in a rugged area that Major Jo Wesley Powell explored in 1869. The si canyons that cut back through the Colora Plateau contain splendid panoramas that can seen from a boat or a lakeside campsite. One these canyons contains the world's large natural bridge, Rainbow Bridge, which is separate national monume*

A FINAL THOUGHT OR TWO

In the United States today we have national parks, historic areas, cultural sites, and recreation areas. Landscapes are ever so subtly changing, historic properties are continually aging and deteriorating, and cultures are altering. We have an unattainable ideal *if* that ideal is to protect, preserve, and present national parks and cultural sites to the public *unchanged* from generation to generation. Change does occur—constantly. Trees grow, plant succession continues, wildlife numbers increase or diminish, exotics appear, conditions fluctuate. The historic scene is marred by intrusive developments; crowds increase; wear and tear occurs. So these factors must be taken into account in policies of management and use.

I first visited Carlsbad Caverns National Park 50 years ago. The comparatively few visitors were organized into groups, each led by a park ranger. One could walk both in and out of the caverns by trail. Evening bat flights were an incredible sight. At the Rock of Ages formation, lights were turned out, making the darkest night one ever experienced, and the old, familiar hymn was sung.

But things have changed at Carlsbad. There are huge crowds, largely self-guided; few bats appear; the lights stay on. There is no song. Ah, but the Caverns and their beautiful formations are seemingly unchanged, and they inspire visitors today just as they did 50 years ago.

Forty years ago I began working at Grand Canyon. By today's standards some of the Canyon's early visitor facilities on the rim are poorly located. But what about Canyon scenery and views of the Canyon from the rims? It is true, there are distractions from aircraft, waiting lists for river and Inner Canyon mule trips, and dozens of other developments and changes that have taken place in the intervening years.

At least two prospects loom large for the future. They can be posed as questions.

Are there too many visitors?

Is the National Park Service showing sufficient concern for natural and cultural resource management?

One hears that "the National Parks are being loved to death." No less an authority than the eminent NPS historian Bill Everhart has suggested

DAVID MUENCH

that such a comment may have been heard first about 1915. In that year the driver of a tallyho stagecoach in Yellowstone encountered his first automobile. It was a 1911 Winton with bicycle wheels and tiller steering, and it almost scared the daylights out of his four-horse team. The elderly driver said to his passengers, "This park as I have known it and loved it is as dead as a dodo." Where there is a problem involving perceived overuse, it almost always centers on the automobile.

Visitors have conflicting expectations. They are usually chagrined to find that so many people have the same idea at the same time of visiting the parks.

Restrict or ration the number of visitors to the parks?

Generally, no. There are too many management options and strategies available: alternate transportation systems, redesigning visitor-service facilities to control capacity at any given time,

ACADIA NATIONAL PARK, Maine. *Once scoured bare by continental glaciation, the region has since clothed its granite mountains and valleys with forests, secluded lakes, and quiet ponds. A rockbound coast adds to the natural beauty. Place-names carry historic reminders of early French and English conflicts for control of the island.*

ARCHES NATIONAL PARK, Utah. *This is red rock country, where wind and water have created more than 200 known sandstone arches of varying sizes and dimensions. Most astounding of these is the fragile-looking, ribbonlike 291-foot span of Landscape Arch. A great assemblage of towers, spires, pinnacles, and balanced rocks complete a beautiful desert landscape.*

reservation and scheduling systems for special activities, changes in advertising and marketing programs within the travel industry, and altering the timing of school vacations.

Not enough concern for natural and cultural resource management?

True. The pace of change quickens. Wildlife population levels are declining in some parks and, conversely, expanding in others. Exotics, both flora and fauna, are competing with or are overwhelming native species.

Developmental and environmental changes affect every unit of the national park system. The greatest single long-range threat to the integrity and continuity of the system is acid rain, affecting vegetation, wildlife, the ecological foundation of the parks, scenic beauty, and all other elements and features contributing to public appreciation and enjoyment. Solution of this problem lies beyond park management and park boundaries.

I firmly believe that overall public support and appreciation of our national parks has never been higher. They will need that continuing support of basic principles if the national park system is to continue to provide enjoyment, understanding, and inspiration into the twenty-first century and beyond.

BIG BEND NATIONAL PARK, Tex. *The park is a land of contrasts and moods. The lofty mile-high green island of the Chisos Mountains creates a sense of solitude. The narrow ribbon of the Rio Grande threads its way through this mountainous region. A teeming green oasis of its own, the river seems quite apart from the arid, fragile Chihuahuan Desert that surrounds and dominates much of the land.*

DAVID MUENCH

OLYMPIC NATIONAL PARK. *Sunsets and seastacks make Olympic's oceanfront a superb visual experience.*

DAVID MUENCH

WOLF TRAP FARM PARK FOR THE PERFORMING ARTS, Va. *Two old barns from up-state New York were brought together at Wolf Trap Farm. Under one roof, with an auditorium designed to seat 400, there was born a facility where cultural offerings from jazz to baroque opera could be presented to the public. Then came disaster in the form of fire. All was destroyed. However, like the phoenix bird, a new facility rose from the ashes of the old.*

EDISON NATIONAL HISTORIC SITE, N.J. *Having his own laboratory with shelves lined with bottles of chemicals and a work table was the dream of a boy not yet ten years old. In later years that dream became a reality for Edison. His fame was to come not in chemistry, however, but from inventions utilizing electricity.*

LYNDON B. JOHNSON NATIONAL HISTORICAL PARK, Tex. *A land of small streams, flower-covered hills, and pleasant valleys with scattered farms, but a land often battered by summer storms and seasonal changes of mood—such is the Hill Country of Texas. This was the region that the thirty-sixth president of the United States loved and where he enjoyed cattle raising and other activities of ranch life. It was to this "Texas White House" that Johnson went when he needed a respite from his heavy official duties.*

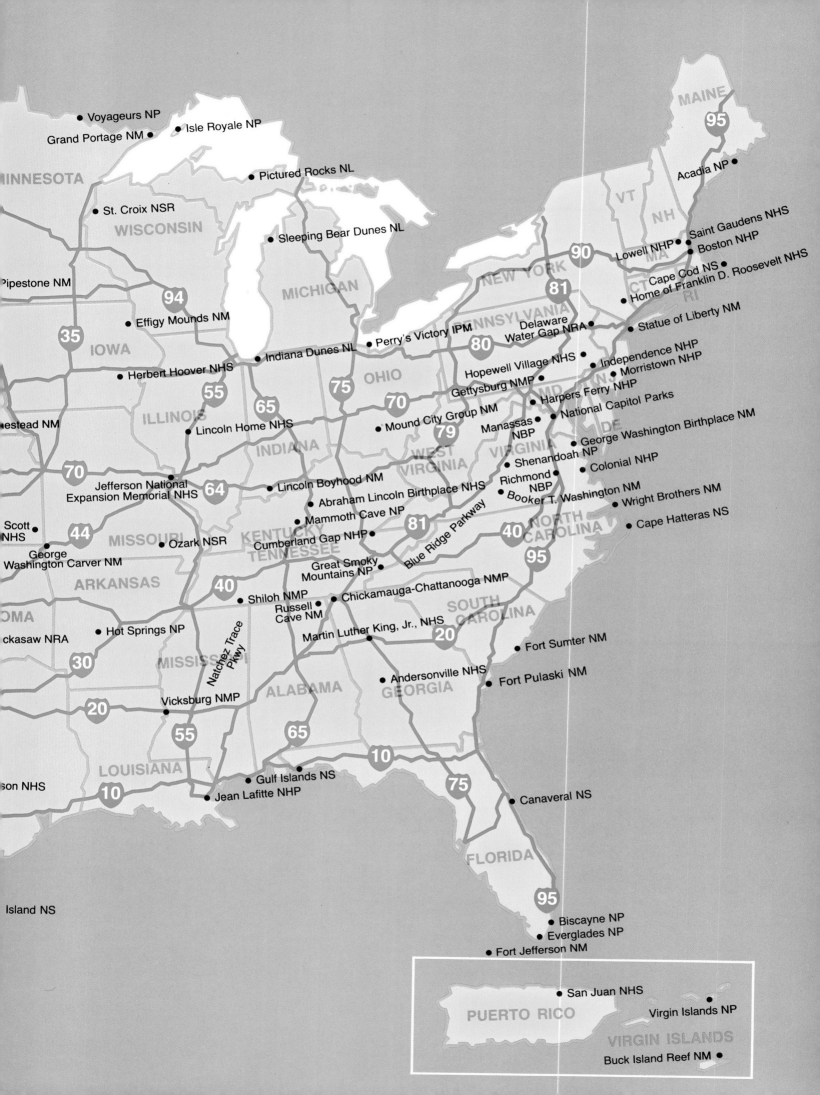

The Future

Bill Mott has *lived* the park system throughout virtually its entire span. He started as a landscape architect the same year Horace Albright retired. Since 1933, park systems have been his way of life. At age 77 he is one of the most dynamic and influential directors the Park Service has ever had.

LINCOLN BOYHOOD NATIONAL MEMORIAL, Ind.
The living history farm recreates pioneer life of the 1820s. Featured at the farm is a replica of the Lincoln cabin, along with other hewn-log buildings such as the smoke house and the carpentry shop. Costumed employees demonstrate daily chores like cooking and spinning.

The future of the national parks lies in the public's understanding of their value. We, the National Park Service, are the stewards of the nation's heritage. It is our job to teach people what values their parks represent. In a rapidly changing world the parks are the constants—the fixed elements of America that can be shared by everyone, not only now but also on into a future we cannot now know or understand.

Just as our fathers could gain inspiration from the awesome splendor of the Grand Canyon and the majesty of Mount McKinley, so can we. And so should our great grandchildren. Nor should we think only of the natural glories of our parks. We hold in trust ancient Indian ruins, the cradles of North American civilization. We assure the preservation of hallowed battlegrounds where a nation was born at Yorktown and Saratoga, and where it grew at Gettysburg and Appomattox. We are today's custodians of the homes of presidents and poets who shaped a nation.

All of these are elements of a national system that, no matter how different the parts, symbolizes the unity of the United States. The future lies in keeping the national park system unified. It is our responsibility to provide our programs with themes so that visitors can better understand the unity the parks represent.

We must make those whose lives have been limited to cities come to realize that a dirt road is not one that needs sweeping, but is a functional element of a Grant-Kohrs Ranch or a Cuyahoga Valley community.

BANDELIER NATIONAL MONUMENT, N.M. *In this canyon, deep and isolated, Pueblo Indian farmers once grew corn, beans, and squash, and along the walls of the gorge they built their masonry villages some with houses three stories high. Magnificient ruins remain to document their presence but leave untold the cause of their abandonment.*

JEFFERSON NATIONAL EXPANSION MEMORIAL NATIONAL HISTORIC SITE, Mo. *Rising 630 feet above its base, the stainless steel arch has been described as "a poetic conquest of space." It is also a colossal "Gateway to the West," symbolizing that period in the life of the nation when all eyes looked westward across the prairies to the Pacific coast.*

By 1840 St. Louis was the "jumping-off place" for would-be emigrants headed westward to the rich prairie lands and to the Pacific. Some stopped along the way to take up ranching, and a cattle industry was born. Others farmed; still more searched the mountains for gold. And finally, many made it into the new lands of Oregon and Washington.

We must assure that the meaning of the heritage is clear to those who visit Hopewell Furnace National Historic Site, Pipestone National Monument, or the monolithic Devil's Tower.

We must be prepared to teach some of the understandings that are lost in the frantic pace of modern life. We need to slow people down, allow their vision to focus on delicate plant life, detailed architectural designs, gentle streams, and silent vistas.

We must draw visitors out of their steel shells, get them to park their cars or drive at a leisurely pace so that they can absorb the special character of the places they visit.

Ours is an era of technology. Although we call it high technology, we might more wisely call it evolving technology, because each passing month finds new potentials and new accomplishments in technology. We will use the innovations and sophistication of this technology to help us do our jobs better. But we must maintain the human element in which person-to-person contact and human scale are available to help defuse the stress and strain of our fast-paced lives.

The parks will face difficulties in the future, just as they have faced them in the past. But we will continue to find ways to surmount those difficulties.

From one generation to the next, from one location to the next, the parks provide continuity. They are sources of inspiration where people come to be refreshed and recharged, physically and spiritually.

It is a measure of America's special greatness that this nation established the first national park and the largest national park system. We have an inheritance that will provide similar experiences for untold future generations. This legacy depends on our sharing the pride and respect we have drawn from the parks with those who will come after us.

Just as the national park system is a product of the nation, its future also depends on the nation. We set the example when we take the time to understand the messages of the parks. We share the natural and cultural heritage they preserve. And we share in their care.

Each of us can pick up a piece of trash. Photograph a flower rather than pick it. Admire the random scattering of petrified wood or lava rocks, but leave them where they were found. We can leave memories, not graffiti. We can set the best example, not follow the worst. Those who would diminish the parks through carelessness or rudeness diminish themselves more.

The future of the parks is a vital element of the future of America. I am confident the Americans know and respect that.

I believe the parks will hold increasing value for our citizens and visitors. With that increased value will come renewed commitment to carry on in the traditions of Horace Albright, Stephen Mather, and others who had the foresight to create this system as we know it today.

DAVID MUENCH

SEQUOIA–KINGS CANYON NATIONAL PARKS, Calif.
There is a feeling of awe and even reverence when one is surrounded by great sequoias that were already giants before recorded history on this continent. To protect and preserve them for future generations was a goal conceived when hundreds of their kind were cut for lumber. That objective was achieved with the creation of these two parks.

Overleaf: PETRIFIED FOREST NATIONAL PARK, Ariz. *A legacy of a once lush world of 225 million years ago, the colorful remains of great conifers in stone remain to tell of ancient forests and of a time when dinosaurs walked the land. Both are part of the fossil history of the park. Photo by Dick Deitrich.*

93

The American bison, more commonly known as the buffalo, is the symbol of the U.S. Department of Interior, within which the National Park Service operates. In the early 1900s the West was a new, unexplored land. A park system was beginning to emerge. Today, virtually the only lands remaining untouched by modernization anywhere in the world are those under the domain of park systems.

Back Cover: FORT CLATSOP NATIONAL MEMORIAL, Oreg. *A small protective log fortification marked the culmination of a memorable journey of discovery by the Lewis and Clark Expedition in 1805. Within this fort, meticulous historical and scientific reports about the journey were written that were to profoundly affect the future of the nation and the Pacific Northwest. Photo by Craig Harmel.*

The publisher gratefully acknowledges the contributions of Duncan Morrow, Marian Schenck, Stanley Paher, and Russ Grater. Russ, who wrote the captions, was the first director of the Harper's Ferry Training Center.

Published by KC Publications · Box 14883 · Las Vegas, NV 89114

Printed by the Krueger Co.
Typography by Stanley Stillion